SO-AMK-942

Challenging Students to Learn

How to Use Effective Leadership and Motivation Tactics

Daniel R. Tomal

Rowman & Littlefield Education
Lanham, Maryland • Toronto • Plymouth, UK
2007

Published in the United States of America
by Rowman & Littlefield Education
A Division of Rowman & Littlefield Publishers, Inc.
A wholly owned subsidiary of The Rowman & Littlefield Publishing Group, Inc.
4501 Forbes Boulevard, Suite 200, Lanham, Maryland 20706
www.rowmaneducation.com

Estover Road
Plymouth PL6 7PY
United Kingdom

British Library Cataloguing in Publication Information Available

Library of Congress Cataloging-in-Publication Data

Tomal, Daniel R.
  Challenging students to learn : how to use effective leadership and motivation
tactics / Daniel R. Tomal.
    p. cm.
  Includes bibliographical references and index.
  ISBN-13: 978-1-57886-591-8 (hardcover : alk. paper)
  ISBN-13: 978-1-57886-592-5 (pbk. : alk. paper)
  ISBN-10: 1-57886-591-3 (hardcover : alk. paper)
  ISBN-10: 1-57886-592-1 (pbk. : alk. paper)
  1. Motivation in education. 2. Effective teaching. 3. Leadership. I. Title.

  LB1065.T595 2007
  370.15'4—dc22   2006037466

⊚™ The paper used in this publication meets the minimum requirements of
American National Standard for Information Sciences—Permanence of Paper
for Printed Library Materials, ANSI/NISO Z39.48-1992.
Manufactured in the United States of America.

Endorsements

"This is a reference that teachers and administrators alike should keep handy on their bookshelf. . . . This is one of those very few books that I will pick up to read again and again." —Robert J Libka, chief education officer, Proviso Township High Schools, Forest Park, Illinois

"I believe all who are involved in the educational community will greatly benefit from this well-written and well-researched book that deals with the 'what' and, more importantly, the 'how to' regarding what is right and makes sense for today's teachers and administrators who are on the line everyday." —C. James Carr, mayor, Wheaton, Illinois; president, Produce Reporter Company; adjunct professor, Wheaton College, Wheaton, Illinois

"*Challenging Students to Learn* is a book that should be required reading by all instructors, administrators, and education students." —Curtis A. Smith, site administrator, Fischler School of Education, Nova Southwestern University, Fort Lauderdale-Davie, Florida

"This book is a sure winner for student enhancement. . . . Strategies for motivating students that educators can effectively use to achieve high academic performance." —Kyle R. Hastings, United States 13th Congressional Democratic State Central Committeeman and mayor, Orland Hills, Illinois

"*Challenging Students to Learn* provides the practitioner with the breadth and depth of both the knowledge and skills necessary to discover and press the magic buttons that will result in the desired developmental outcomes of the students. I recommend this book to any professional who wishes to connect with their students and enhance their ability to grow mentally, emotionally, and physically." —John F. Cindric Jr., professor, College of Education, University of Findlay, Ohio

Contents

Foreword

As the chief education officer of a large urban high school district, I have to say that motivation of students is a top priority at our district. Whether as consultants, administrators, teachers, or parents, we all agree that student motivation is a key factor for student success. What motivates teachers and students is as varied as their teaching and learning styles. This is as true in our new mathematics and science academy for academically talented students as it is in our two traditional high schools. As I begin my 32nd year as an educational leader committed to continual improvement, I welcome thoughtful guidance in these areas and celebrate the development of new resources.

What a pleasure it is to stroll through the pages of this new book. Simultaneously practical and powerful, succinct and broad in its relevant applications, this reference is one that teachers and administrators alike should keep handy on their bookshelves. The essential elements of several graduate courses have been captured and packaged into a compendium of simple strategies and useful tools.

The original inventories and surveys are relevant for either staff development workshops or individual professional growth activities. I have already taken the leadership stress assessment, and I appreciate the stressor categories, which help one to focus on a particular area of stress while considering the best strategy to reduce stress. Chapter 8, "101 Ways to Motivate Students," is a marvelously comprehensive list of strategies for any situation that a teacher might encounter.

Finally, the detailed table of contents makes retrieval of ideas very easy. This is one of those very few books that I will pick up to read again and again. On behalf of those who will read this book, I am confident that it will contribute a positive impact on our work.

Robert J. Libka
Chief Education Officer
Proviso Township High Schools, Forest Park, Illinois

Preface

The ability to lead and motivate students is one of the most difficult jobs of a teacher. Teachers often have students who are apathetic, do not have confidence, or lack enthusiasm to perform to the best of their ability. Teachers need to employ the most effective strategies to help lead and motivate these students. The strategies described in this book are based on years of study, research, and in-service training programs on the topic of leadership and motivation. The book includes many strategies that have been successful in both education and business. Many of the management strategies used to lead and motivate business employees can be useful in leading and motivating students. These strategies can be effective for public and private elementary and secondary schools and in university settings for teacher preparation programs. They are practical and useful techniques that can be used by any educator. These strategies can also help teachers to motivate students to perform academically, improve their behavior in the classroom, and develop better attitudes toward school and learning. Moreover, leading and motivating students can be a fun and satisfying experience for any educator in incorporating the strategies and seeing the positive results.

The first chapter provides the principles and history of leadership and motivation. The chapter includes the topics of power and leadership, quality leaders, teamwork, and proactive leadership and how they affect the leadership and motivation of students. This chapter also includes the popular theories of situational leadership, the X and Y model, the leadership grid, and total quality management.

Chapter 2 is a critical chapter in that it provides many of the leadership strategies that have been found to be successful in business and have now been adapted for educators. Some of the strategies include Maslow's hierarchy, Alderfer's model, expectancy model, two-factor motivational theory, the equity motivation model, Theory Z, team leadership, and proactive leadership. Practical examples of these theories are given throughout the chapter.

Chapter 3 is a comprehensive chapter that concentrates on the area of motivating students. Several theories of motivation are described, such as the leadership capability model, values and culture, SMART criteria, the self-fulfilling prophecy, and other human-needs-based strategies. Examples of applying these motivational theories in the educational setting are given and compared to those of the business world. Several case studies and illustrations are provided to assist educators in applying these strategies in the classroom. The chapter also includes a comprehensive motivational study.

Chapter 4 presents the topic of communicating with students. The basic model of communication is provided as a foundation in understanding communication among people. The topics of verbal and nonverbal communication and the importance of interpersonal communication are provided. An important feature of this chapter includes the use of personality styles and how understanding and using appropriate styles can enhance leadership and motivation. The chapter concludes with the topic of active listening. An important aspect of leading and motivating students is a teacher's ability to actively listen to students. Several strategies in active listening and conducting counseling sessions are presented in this chapter.

The fifth chapter describes how to motivate students through appropriate classroom management and negotiations. Several areas in classroom management, such as lesson planning, engaging students, principles of motivation, negotiations, and tactics, are described in this chapter. Moreover, the uses of negotiating tactics to motivate students are presented.

Chapter 6 covers the area of discipline and teacher countertactics as they relate to leading and motivating students. Several methods of discipline are provided, and emphasis is given to the advanced technique of discipline by negotiations. The chapter concludes with lessons on how to create win-win situations and implement discipline models within the classroom.

The seventh chapter deals with leading and motivating students in special situations. Topics of teamwork and collaboration, managing conflict, and stress are covered as they relate to student motivation. This chapter also includes the topic of legal considerations, to help the teacher understand his or her rights as well as the rights of students in leadership and motivation.

The last chapter presents a unique collection of 101 ways to motivate students. These strategies are practical and proven methods to help all educators. Categories include tangible rewards, intangible rewards, instructional strategies, classroom management, and building positive relationships.

FEATURES OF THE BOOK

Nothing can be worse than reading a book that is boring, dry, and impractical for educators. This book is unique in that it provides many colorful examples that can be used by all educators. One of the most valuable features of the book is the incorporation of many diverse strategies related to leading, motivating, communicating, disciplining, and managing the classroom. They are provided in a straightforward and practical manner. The topics in this book can also be useful for administrators in employing workable institutional programs and teacher in-service sessions.

Other features of this book include

- Strategies for leading and motivating students in the school environment
- Models of leadership and motivational theories that have been proven in the business world, as applied to the educational setting
- A comprehensive description of how to apply leadership and motivational theories
- Real situations that have been successfully applied within the classroom
- Up-to-date guidelines, school policies, and legal considerations
- Practical strategies in giving student feedback and taking action for improvement
- Examples of stressful situations and how to manage stress
- A review of some of the major discipline theories and models

- Strategies in managing conflict and how to promote teamwork and collaboration
- Strategies in conducting a coaching session

The strategies for leading and motivating students presented in this book are based on years of conducting in-service teacher workshops and classroom sessions at the university level. For example, using intrinsic and extrinsic motivational factors, supplying reinforcement, maintaining good classroom management, engaging students, incorporating effective instruction and curriculum, and exercising fair discipline are just some of the factors covered in this book. Their advantages and disadvantages are discussed, and examples are given where these strategies have been applied in schools.

Although there are many books written on education, there are not many books that are devoted to leading and motivating students. Therefore, one unique factor of this book is the concentration of leading and motivating teaching techniques that can be used to achieve high academic performance. Strategies in obtaining good student behavior and moral character are also covered.

This book also contains a rich source of educational and reference materials so that educators can apply the concepts for leading and motivating students. These materials include

- Case illustrations and figures in applying leadership and motivation strategies
- Several ideas for giving tangible rewards
- Several ideas for giving intrinsic rewards
- Examples of motivation strategies that have improved academic performance
- A sample of field-based educational issues
- Actual examples of assessments used in assessing and motivating students

Last, the book provides a fascinating chapter on 101 ways to motivate students. Some of these strategies are in the areas of

- Providing tangible and intangible rewards
- Communicating effectively with students

- Using effective instructional techniques
- Reducing stress and conflict
- Building positive relationships
- Maintaining a positive classroom environment

ORGANIZATION OF THE BOOK

This book is organized in a straightforward manner so that educators can understand the basic theories and strategies in leading and motivating students. Each chapter builds on the previous one; however, each chapter is also distinct because it covers a specific topic that relates to leading and motivating students. Last, each chapter includes basic theories and examples of applying these theories in the educational setting.

Acknowledgments

Appreciation is extended to the many people who have assisted and worked with me. Special appreciation is given to my students, colleagues, and former business associates in the corporate world. Thanks to Susan Webb for typing the manuscript and Annette and Justin Tomal for reviewing the manuscript. I also wish to recognize and extend appreciation to the many schools and districts where I have worked and given seminars, such as the Chicago Public Schools, Bellwood School District 88, Cicero School District 99, Lake Central School Corporation, Proviso Township High Schools, West Chicago District 33, School District 131, Michigan City Township High Schools, Findlay Schools, Arai School, Armstrong School, Aurora High School, Boone School, College of DuPage, Field School, Glenbrook High School, Harper College, Kilmer School, Jordan School, McCutcheon School, Newfield School, Oakton College, Proviso Area for Exceptional Children, Passages School, Park Forest Schools, Rogers Park Cluster, Rogers School, Sayre Academy, St. Giles Academy, Stewart School, Stockton School, Triton College, Uptown Cluster, Walt Disney School, Waubonsee College, Concordia University, and Lutheran Church Missouri Synod schools. Last, I wish to extend gratitude to the people who endorsed this book and provided insight for the project.

1

Leading Students

LEADERSHIP PERSPECTIVE

Being an effective leader is an important responsibility for every teacher. One of the most important jobs that a person can have is that of a teacher who leads his or her students in becoming successful social citizens. Therefore, teachers have a responsibility to try to make a positive impact on all students whom they encounter in their classrooms. As Starratt (2004) states,

> educational leaders must be morally responsible, not only in preventing and alleviating harm but also in a proactive sense of who the leader is, what the leader is responsible as, whom the leader is responsible to, and what the leader is responsible for. (p. 49)

So, what makes an effective leader? Much like a manager in a company, a teacher needs to have many management qualities (e.g., organizing work, managing time and resources) as well as the tools to inspire people to accomplish the leader's vision and goals.

Poor leaders can have damaging effects on students. For example, ineffective leaders who belittle and demotivate their students can cause psychological and academic harm to students. Moreover, when poor leaders are unorganized and exhibit poor time management, these behaviors can result in an ineffective learning environment. Students often become frustrated and demotivated with disorganized leaders, just like workers do in the business world.

There are many qualities of effective educational leaders, such as having technical academic knowledge, interpersonal skills, and the ability to establish a clear educational vision for their students. Good leaders may not always possess exceptional intelligence, but they are able to inspire others to accomplish academic and behavioral goals. For example, one of the qualities of an effective leader is the ability to establish a clear-cut vision for his or her students. A vision is a concrete plan that is different from a mission. A mission is a general statement such as "to explore the galaxies." A vision is much more concrete, such as "to land a man on the moon and watch him walk." Effective leaders have the ability to establish a clear-cut vision for their students in terms of academic and behavioral performance. They know how to measure the results of their vision.

Once a vision is established by an effective educator, he or she must have the ability to inspire students to share the same vision and be committed to accomplishing the vision. So, in essence, effective leaders are people who are able to establish a vision and then accomplish the vision through their students.

Another characteristic of an effective leader is that of role modeling. Good leaders often become good role models for their students so that these students can model after the good leader and develop these same traits. Good followers often make good leaders. The ability to effectively inspire students and then to exhibit effective leadership characteristics is critical in educating and modeling these characteristics for students. For example, if an ineffective leader demonstrates poor characteristics, such as temper tantrums and impatience, these poor traits may be adapted by their students. Therefore, the importance of being a good role model for students is critical, especially for the developmental years.

Effective leaders also have the ability to use their power in the most effective manner. There are several types of power that a teacher possesses, such as legitimate power, expert power, political power, and reverence power (French & Bell, 1995). For example, teachers possess legitimate power because of the authority vested in their position as a teacher. This legitimate power allows the teacher to administer punishment as well as rewards. Expert power is a form of power given a teacher by his or her mere virtue of understanding the content better than the students do. By having expert power, the teacher gains power over the students and, often, respect. Political power comes from the teacher's ability to work with people in social systems and to gain support from his or her colleagues, students, parents, and community. Reverence power is the ability to gain respect and power because of the teacher's own personality. Some people, because of their actions and behaviors, command different degrees of reverence power. This reverence power may be a result of being charismatic.

Although good leaders may be able to use legitimate power of punishment, they would be more effective when using the power of reverence. If teachers use the power of reverence rather than the threat of punishment, they are more apt to gain respect and build confidence and motivation in their students.

SITUATIONAL LEADERSHIP

One of the more popular leadership theories was developed by Hersey and Blanchard (1977), titled situational leadership. This theory builds on the situational leadership styles proposed by authors who developed a continuum of leadership behavior ranging from authoritarian (tell) to delegating (see Figure 1.1). The situational leadership theory is applicable to the educational setting. This theory can be valuable in helping teachers understand the best styles in leading their students. To understand this theory, there are several terms that need to be defined. *Task behavior* can be defined as one-way communication (directive behavior) from a teacher to a student. When a teacher uses task behavior, he or she is giving direct instructions to a student. The task behavior is directive, and there is no interchange or conversation. In this style, the student is basically listening to the teacher.

The term *relationship behavior* can be described as two-way communication between a teacher and student. The relationship behavior is supportive, and this communication is considered to be two-way discussion. This behavior also assumes that there is a high emphasis on both talking and listening.

The term *maturity* can be described as the degree of a student's positive attitude, experience, and overall emotional maturity toward the teacher. The maturity level ranges from low to moderate to high. If a student has low maturity, he or she is considered to be immature. A high maturity level describes a student as being mature in his or her attitude and behavior toward the teacher.

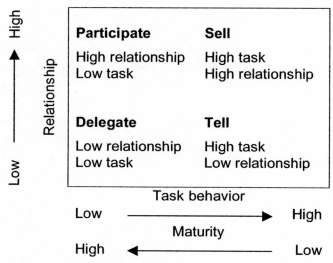

Figure 1.1.   Situational Leadership Model
Source: Hersey and Blanchard (1977).

The situational leadership model comprises four leadership styles. The first style is called *telling*. In this style, the teacher uses a high-task and a low-relationship behavior. An example is that of when a teacher is giving one-way instruction to the student and there is virtually no discussion. The second style is called *selling*. This style uses high-task and high-relationship behaviors. In this style the teacher is engaging in directive conversation with a student. This style considers that the maturity level of the student is between low and moderate. The next leadership style is called *participating*. In this style, the teacher uses high-relationship and low-task behaviors. This leadership style assumes that the maturity level of the student is increasing, and it ranges between moderate and high. The last leadership style is called *delegating*. This style uses low-relationship and low-task behaviors. It also assumes that the maturity level of the student is high.

Let's examine an example of how a teacher can use the situational leadership theory in leading a student. If a teacher has a new student enrolled in the classroom, the teacher can assume that the student most likely has a low maturity level, given that he or she does not know the rules of the classroom. In this situation, the teacher may begin using the telling style. The telling style assumes that the student knows little about the classroom operations; therefore, the teacher needs to exhibit high-task and low-relationship behaviors. The teacher begins by explaining the rules and procedures of the classroom while the student listens. There is no need for two-way discussion, given that the student at the beginning has a primary need to gain information. The teacher should not assume that the telling style is an ineffective style; rather, it can be appropriate for a new student who has a low maturity level.

As the student begins to mature and starts to understand the rules and procedures of the classroom, there becomes a need for high-task and high-relationship behavior by the teacher. In this situation the teacher uses the selling style. This style assumes that there is two-way conversation with the student. For example, the student might begin to ask questions and participate in conversation with the teacher, even though the teacher still needs to be fairly directive in explaining the operations of the classroom.

As the new student continues to mature and develops more of a moderate-to-high maturity level, the teacher can then use the participating style. The participating style assumes that there is a need for high-relationship and low-task behaviors. In this situation the teacher needs to continue to give respect to the student by embarking in a two-way conversation, given that there is little need for the teacher to be directive.

As the student continues to mature and develops a high maturity level, the teacher can then use the delegating style. In this situation there is a need for low-relationship and low-task behaviors. When the student has a high maturity level, the teacher no longer needs to explain the rules and operations of the classroom because the student knows them and is mature and respectful of them. The example of a new student and his or her maturity development provides an effective situation for a teacher to utilize all four styles of situational leadership in an appropriate manner. Although variations may occur in the student's maturity level, the teacher should constantly be aware of assessing this maturity level and adapt his or her leadership style appropriately.

The situational leadership model considers three major aspects—the style of the leader, the students being lead, and the situation. For example, the situational leadership model does not indicate that there is only one right style; rather, the model suggests that the teacher should use the appropriate style given the situation and maturity level of the students. For example, if a teacher is conducting a lesson during the class period and a student engages in highly disruptive behavior, the teacher should most likely resort to the telling leadership style and be directive in asking the student to behave. The telling style is often appropriate when a teacher needs quick directive change in a student's misbehavior. Another example where the telling style may be appropriate is in the case of an emergency. If there is a fire drill, and directive instructions need to be given to students for their welfare, the teacher should use the telling style. During an emergency situation, there is generally no need for two-way discussion; rather, the teacher needs to act decisively in ensuring the safety of the students and give one-way instruction.

The selling situation leadership style is one that a teacher may find useful in persuading students to improve their study habits. For example, a teacher who uses the telling style to improve a student's study habits may cause the student to become resentful because of the teacher's directive behavior. The selling style may be best in that the teacher uses a conversational two-way discussion and acts firm and directive in the importance of maintaining good study habits.

The participating leadership style can be effective when dealing with students who have a moderate-to-high maturity level. For example, if a teacher has students who have a positive attitude and are willing to learn, the two-way conversation may be the best leadership style. In this situation, the teacher is more apt to encourage the student to become engaged with the learning process through his or her participation and discussion with the teacher.

The delegating leadership style can be effective when dealing with students who have a high maturity level. For example, if students are working on a classroom project and understand the method in completing it, then the teacher may need to give little instruction. The students have a positive attitude and know how to perform the project; they just need to complete it. The teacher in this situation may not need to engage in discussion with the student but can delegate the project and allow the students to work together and complete it. The delegation style can be effective in allowing high-maturity students to make decisions without interaction with the teacher.

The main aspect of using situational leadership includes the notion that the teacher needs to use the most effective style given the situation. For example, a teacher may have used the delegation style with a student who has a high maturity level. However, if the student begins to lose his or her maturity level and slips to a low level, then the teacher may need to adjust his or her style accordingly. In this case, if the student now has a low maturity level and begins disruptive behavior with his or her fellow students, the teacher may need to adapt the telling style to best lead the student.

There are many situations in which the teacher can use the situational leadership model outside the classroom. For example, when a teacher interacts with students in the hallway, any of these four styles may be appropriate. The teacher may need to use the telling style to tell a student to report to a classroom, or the teacher may need to engage the selling style if he or she needs to be directive and engage in two-way conversation. If a student has a moderate maturity level and is in need of advice and counsel from a teacher, the teacher may then utilize the participating style in this situation. Last, if the students are passing in the hallway between classes appropriately, then the teacher can use a delegating style, given that there is no need to intervene. Understanding the appropriate use of each of these styles can be effective for a teacher in leading his or her students.

Another way of understanding and applying this model is in regard to a further understanding of the maturity level of students. A low maturity level suggests that students may be unable, unwilling, or insecure about their learning. There are many reasons why the student may have this attitude. This maturity level can be referred to as the *readiness of the student*. Low-maturity students are simply unable to sufficiently learn because of their insecurity or poor attitude. However, on the other end of the continuum, a high-maturity student is able, willing, and confident in his or her ability (i.e., the student can be viewed as having a high readiness, or a high maturity level).

A unique aspect of applying the situational leadership theory is its dynamic aspect. The teacher may find himself or herself simultaneously using the telling, selling, participating, and delegating styles in the classroom on a frequent basis. The teacher may be using one-way directive (telling) behavior with a student and then immediately switch to a participating style with other students. The teacher's ability to quickly switch the styles within the classroom is key in successfully applying this theory. One danger for a teacher who is using this style is that of becoming overly dependent on it. A teacher may become trapped in consistently using the telling style, but this style will most likely not be effective in dealing with all students all the time. Likewise, if the teacher uses only the delegating style, this can have devastating consequences. Students who need direction may resort to misbehavior and limited learning given that they need interaction from the teacher.

POSITIVE LEADERSHIP

One of the landmark theories in developing positive leadership was proposed by McGregor (1960). He proposed a theory that centers on the attitude of the leader. He suggested that leaders largely fall into one of two styles—that under Theory X or Theory Y—as described in Table 1.1.

McGregor believed that leaders tend to make assumptions about their followers. For example, he thought that a Theory X leader assumes that people are lazy and irresponsible and that they need to be coerced, controlled, and directed in order to perform work. He believed that Theory X leaders view their workers as people who inherently dislike work and have little ambition.

The Theory Y leader exhibits the opposite traits and assumptions than does the Theory X leader. The Theory Y leader believes that people are creative, self-directed, desire to work, are responsible, and find fulfillment in their work. Essentially, McGregor believed that the Theory X leader is negative, and the Theory Y leader positive, toward people.

McGregor's theory has wide implications for leading students. For example, if a teacher posits the Theory X assumption, then the teacher tends to be directive and threatening to his or her students. These teachers often develop a sarcastic attitude toward their students. The students, in turn, often behave and perform accordingly. In other words, if you don't expect much, you don't get much. If people are treated as if they are lazy and irresponsible, then they often perform to the leader's expectations. Although some teachers may not vividly exhibit Theory X behavior, students can pick up on subtle cues from the leader. For example, the teacher may have less eye contact with students, exhibit a frown, or use a vocal inflection that suggests that the teacher has negative assumptions about

Table 1.1.   Leadership Styles Under Theory X and Theory Y

Theory X Leader	Leader Y Leader
Dislikes work	Work is natural
Avoids work	Is productive
Needs to be coerced	Seeks work
Needs to be controlled	Seeks responsibility
Needs to be directed	Seeks learning
Needs to be threatened	Desires advancement
Not self-motivated	Is self-motivated

Source: Adapted from McGregor (1960).

his or her students. Moreover, the subtle use of a teacher's nonverbals can be revealing. For example, if a teacher tends to point his or her finger and talk in a condescending manner toward the students, these cues become obvious and reveal the teacher's true assumptions.

The Theory Y teacher is one who exhibits a positive attitude toward his or her students. This teacher promotes a healthy atmosphere and motivates students to perform their best. The teacher's assumption is to expect the best of the students, and students, in turn, will often perform to expectations.

The most important significance of McGregor's theory is that the assumptions that teachers as leaders have toward their students can create a self-fulfilling prophecy. The notion of the self-fulfilling prophecy is that a belief in an event or expectation can actually cause it to happen. Therefore, if leaders do not expect much from their students, they will not get much. On the other hand, if leaders place high expectations on students, then students will perform to their high expectations. The concept of self-fulfilling prophecy can be seen in many aspects of life. In the sports arena, the concept of the self-fulfilling prophecy is widely used. If a coach places high expectations on his or her players, the players will often perform to those expectations. For example, if a coach removes a player from the game at a critical moment because he or she does not believe that the player can succeed and thus replaces the player with another player, these expectations can have reinforcing consequences. The player who is removed will often continue to perform less, whereas the player in whom the coach has confidence often improves his or her performance. The essence is that success has reinforcing consequences. The notion that success breeds success is supportive of the self-fulfilling prophecy. Therefore, whether the leader is a coach leading a sports team or a teacher leading a group of students, the same concepts apply.

THE LEADERSHIP GRID

Another popular and classic leadership model is the theory called the *leadership grid*, by Blake and Mouton (1969; see Figure 1.2). The leadership grid describes five leadership styles. The general notion of this grid implies that all leaders make assumptions regarding concern for production versus concern for people. Concern for production implies that leaders have a

high task-directive desire for obtaining productivity. These leaders place a
higher value on achieving productivity versus that of being concerned for
people. The lefthand side of the grid describes a scale for the leader's concern for people. A low concern for people scores a 1, whereas a high concern for people scores a 9. In this model the relationship between concern
for production and concern for people can then be plotted on the grid. The
authors have devised instruments that measure a leader's concern for production and people and the resultant dominant style.

The Abdicator Leader

The *abdicator leader* is one who exerts minimum effort and concern to either people or production. He or she does not have regard for getting work
accomplished, nor does he or she have much care for the feelings of people. This type of leader can sometimes be viewed as being apathetic and
ineffective. For example, if a teacher is suffering from burnout and has
negative feelings toward the school system and dislikes his or her students, he or she may adapt the style of the abdicator leader. This type of
teacher may be resentful toward both the students and the school and is
simply waiting out his or her time to retire. This type of leader can be
damaging to students. Generally, this type of leader does not receive much
respect, nor does he or she produce a healthy learning environment. The
abdicator leader scores a 1.1 on the leadership grid. This style indicates
low concern for people and production.

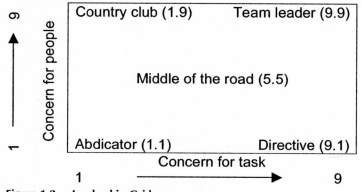

Figure 1.2.   Leadership Grid
Source: Based on Blake and Mouton (1985).

The Country Club Leader

The *country club leader* is a manager who scores a 1.9 on the leadership grid. This type of leader has a high concern for people but a low concern for production. This leader is more concerned about satisfying the needs of people than about getting results. For example, this type of leader may give exceptionally high grades to all students in an effort to stay in their favor. Another typical example of this type of leader may be a new teacher who desires to have the respect of all of his or her students and be accepted by them. Although this type of leader may succeed in obtaining many friendships, he or she probably does not produce an enriching learning environment. As a consequence, the students probably do not achieve at their highest level. Another example of the country club leader is a situation where a teacher receives many complaints from students and parents and feels that his or her job is in jeopardy, so he or she resorts to being overly friendly to his or her students. Although the country club leader may not be as bad as the abdicator leader, this style is nevertheless ineffective in achieving the best results from students.

The Middle-of-the-Road Leader

The *middle-of-the-road leader* scores a 5.5 on the leadership grid. This type of leader tends to have a balance between wanting to satisfy the needs of people and getting results. This type of leader can sometimes be viewed as straddling the fence because the leader has only moderate concern toward people and production. An example of this leader is a teacher who simply views his or her job as only a job and places only moderate effort in the concern for people or production.

The Directive Leader

The *directive leader* is one who is most interested in getting results and has little regard to satisfy the needs of people. For example, this type of leader is a teacher who is concerned only with getting high test scores at the expense of jeopardizing student relationships. This teacher tends to be directive and not very friendly toward students. Although this type of leader is striving to obtain high test scores, the result may be less, given his or her authoritarian style.

The Team Leader

The *team leader* scores a 9.9 on the leadership grid. This type of leader has a high concern for people as well as that for production. Blake and Mouton (1969) believe that this is the ideal style and that all leaders should strive to be the team leader. This style encourages work being accomplished through committed people who have trust and respect for one another. The authors emphasized that all leaders should strive to obtain the team leader style and that this can be a growing process as the leader matures and becomes experienced.

The leadership grid has wide implications for the educational field. This model can easily be applied for teachers in obtaining effective leadership skills in managing their students. Teachers should strive to become a team leader.

QUALITY LEADERSHIP

In the 1980s the United States experienced a transformation in conducting business. Manufacturing had been experiencing poor quality in America. In an effort to address this problem, the *total quality management* (TQM) initiative arose. TQM was coined by the U.S. Department of Defense (Ciampa, 1992). The essence of TQM is to meet or exceed customers' expectations. TQM is a philosophy that centers on quality leadership. Some characteristics of TQM include teamwork, continual improvement, quality excellence, quality of work life, honesty and trust, mutual respect and dignity, employee responsibility, integrity, and customer focus.

The essence of a quality leader is one who places high value on his or her people and encourages creativity, self-initiative, trust, and empowerment. The quality leader continually tries to improve teamwork and a positive organizational culture. Quality leadership replaced the old concept that people must be highly supervised and given individual responsibility for performing job tasks. Quality leadership places emphasis on group teamwork, creativity, and concern for the total product versus individual tasks. The old concept of leadership considered the leader as an authoritarian who was in charge of people and given a title such as *president*, *principal*, *director*, or *vice president*. The philosophy of TQM views the leader as a servant leader within the organization serving his or her people. Customers are placed at the top of the organization, versus the old vertical management system of the president or principal being at the top of the organization. TQM attempts to break down barriers, and it often removes titles and refers to people as *associates*. Vice presidents and supervisors are often called *coaches* or *team leaders*. The idea is to promote teamwork versus hierarchical division.

Other characteristics of quality leaders include those of participation, facilitation, coordination, and coaching. These leaders are viewed as taking a consulting role and trying to delegate responsibility to their team members. These leaders encourage innovation and risk taking. Ciampa (1992) defines TQM as "a total dedication to the customer—a mindset totally dedicated to the customer's satisfaction in every way possible" (p. 6). The overall objective of TQM is to meet or exceed customers' expectations through shared values and teamwork, as described as follows:

- Customer satisfaction and loyalty
- Cheaper, faster, better
- Continual improvement
- Motivated teamwork through employee involvement
- Leadership support for people
- Minimum response time in solving problems
- Recognizing and taking advantage of learning opportunities

One of the leading pioneers of the TQM philosophy was W. Edwards Deming. Trained as a physicist, Deming achieved significant recognition for his contributions in rebuilding Japanese industry after World War II. Deming is well known for his creation of the 14 points for effective organizations. Some of his points include driving out fear, eliminating slogans, removing barriers for pride in workmanship, and constantly improving quality and learning in leadership. The nature of Deming's points can be applied to educational leaders. For example, if a teacher can attempt to drive out fear and allow his or her students to be creative without the threat of a poor grade, students may achieve more. Deming was not a proponent of issuing grades to students and believed that the love of learning was most important. The teacher who adapts many of the principles of TQM may promote a classroom that has a common vision, shared

values, and teamwork. Many of these principles can serve students well
and allow for optimum learning and personal growth in the classroom.
The adoption of TQM leadership qualities requires a positive attitude,
good behaviors, and commitment. Some leadership values include the following:

- Student focused
- High ethics
- Honesty and trust
- Mutual respect and dignity
- Student responsibility
- Innovation and vitality
- Fairness

- Engagement
- Social responsibility
- Self-efficacy
- Collaboration
- Creativity
- Mutual support
- High integrity

Some examples of that contrast between the traditional leader and the
quality leader include the following:

Traditional Leader
- Control
- Intimidation
- Strict discipline
- Telling
- Blaming
- Directing
- Critical
- Compliance

Quality Leader
- Collaborative
- Accountability
- Responsibility
- Engaging
- Innovative
- Empowering
- Motivating
- Group-centered

The quality leader must understand that TQM requires patience and a
long-term commitment. Quality leaders need to understand that it is easy
to slip back into the traditional method of supervision rather than be disciplined in practicing the qualities of TQM leadership.

Several methods to kill quality leadership are described as follows:

- Perceiving TQM as magic versus a philosophy
- Failing to create learning vision
- Expecting short-term miracles
- Lacking a reward system

- Lacking genuine support and standards
- Hindering creativity and innovation
- Failing to walk the talk
- Failing to forgive mistakes
- Lacking continual improvement
- Failing to employ authentic assessment

TEAM LEADERSHIP

An effective leader is one who promotes a team concept in the classroom. For example, the teacher can consider the students in the classroom as his or her team. The students who make up the team all have individual strengths and talents and can develop these strengths through team exercises. If the students do not feel connected with their fellow classmates (i.e., team), they will not achieve to their fullest potential. Wagner and Kegan (2006) reinforce the team concept by stating, "Communities of practice are characterized by a shared passion, commitment, and identification with a group's purpose. They promote engagement by providing forums for professionals to learn, grow, and become more effective at their craft" (p. 75). The classroom is one large team in which the students should have positive feelings toward one another as team members. A team that has negative attributes, such as jealousy, negativism, excessive competition, and negative rivalry, can hinder both individual and team performance. Negative team behaviors can distract students from performing to their best level. Therefore, the teacher, as the instructional leader, should develop the team aspects of the students for optimum performance.

Tuckman (1965) identifies four stages of team development: forming, storming, conforming, and performing. Teachers can consider these stages of development in promoting positive teamwork within the classroom. The forming stage can be considered the honeymoon stage. Students are generally guarded, exchange pleasantries, and are somewhat respectful and cordial to one another. In this first stage, students are still assessing their environment and the personalities of their classmates. Students experience a degree of uncertainty regarding their relationships with their fellow classmates and assess the degree in which they have positive relationships.

In the second stage, storming, conflicts emerge and classmates bid for power. They often rebel against their leader as well as their fellow classmates in an effort to gain power and recognition. The students are attempting to find their places within the team, or a sense of unwritten social order. Students who emerge as winners develop informal power and leadership positions within the classroom.

The third stage, conforming, is sometimes referred to as the norming stage. This stage includes students who establish standards of conduct and set norms for behavior. During this stage, students, for the most part, accept these rules and standards; however, they may still lack open support of one another.

The last stage, performing, is when the group is a highly functioning and proficient team. This stage allows group members to feel supportive of one another, develop a sense of loyalty, and manage conflicts constructively. When the leader is able to help a team achieve the highest level of performing, team members feel free to grow and learn and experiment with new learning experiences. It is at this stage where the group functions most productively and efficiently. The feelings of students during this stage are positive toward one another. Students generally have a sense of *we* and collaboration with one another. Much like teammates on a good sports team, students have feelings toward their team members that are cooperative and supportive as they all pursue a common goal (i.e., learning and development). A highly functioning team that achieves the stage of performing may also go through a stage of mourning when it disbands, such as in the case of moving to the next grade level or graduating.

The leader can help the team members achieve the performing stage through clear rules of conduct, a common purpose, trust and honesty, commitment, effective communications, appropriate conflict management, and recognition and reward systems. The leader is, in essence, the person who lays the tracks and sets the example for the students to follow. The old expression "You can lead a horse to water, but you can't make it drink" is appropriate in that the leader cannot force the students to become highly functioning team members, but he or she can provide situations that allow the students to achieve high-performance teamwork.

One of the elements of promoting effective team functioning is that of collaboration and cooperation. Cooperative learning is not a new strategy. Cooperative learning has been used to support growth and development at almost every grade level and every subject area. Cooperative learning can allow face-to-face interaction among team members in problem-solving and decision-making activities. Both individual and group accountability can be accomplished through cooperative learning as well. Individuals need to be held accountable to their team members as well as to the group. Cooperative learning can produce synergistic results in that the whole can be greater than the sum of the individual contributions. Group members can also encourage each of the team members to contribute during cooperative learning exercises. For example, one popular cooperative learning strategy is called *think-pair-share* (Amends, 2003). In this process, the teacher introduces a question and then requires the students to individually reflect on it. Then the teacher pairs off the students and asks that they discuss the question collectively. After a period, the leader then asks a spokesperson from each of the pairs to share the pair's ideas and answers with the entire class.

In promoting team development, the teacher needs to provide a clear and common structure for rules of conduct. Group members need to know behavior expectations as well as consequences for poor behavior. Essentially, the teacher lays the ground rules for the classroom. In addition to citing behavioral expectations, the leader should also define clear standards of performance. Students, as long as they believe that these rules and expectations are reasonable, will generally accept them as long as they are administered consistently. In addition to providing role clarity, the goals for academic achievement need to be defined. These goals are often based on identified learning standards so that students can understand the results.

Another important element of building teamwork is for the group to have a common set of core values. When a leader acquires a new team (e.g. class), one of the first exercises that could be conducted is that of a team values (see Figure 1.3). In this exercise the leader can ask the students to rank 10 values from 1 to 10 (1 being most important and 10 being least important) describing what they need from each of their classmates to achieve a highly functioning successful team. After the students have completed the individual rankings, they can work in small groups to collaboratively complete their rankings. Upon completion of the small-group rankings, the leader can conduct discussion as a large group and determine the overall ranking of team values for the class. It is important that

Directions: Rank these values from 1 to 10 (1 being most important and 10 being least important) indicating what you need from each of your classmates for your class to be successful as a team. The first column is for individual students, the second for small groups.

Power and authority	_____	_____
Fairness	_____	_____
Achievement	_____	_____
Honesty and trust	_____	_____
Creativity	_____	_____
Integrity	_____	_____
Tolerance	_____	_____
Loyalty	_____	_____
Respect	_____	_____
Responsibility	_____	_____

Figure 1.3.   Team Values Survey

the class, as a team, develop consensus. In this exercise, teams often identify honesty and trust as the most important values. Without honesty and trust, many students believe that they cannot achieve well as a team or be fair to one another. Power and authority are often ranked last in this exercise. Although there may be individual differences in the rankings of these values, it is important for a team to develop a common set of values from which to operate.

Communication is another critical element for developing teamwork. The teacher needs to provide clear instructions for daily activities, and this should be done in both written and oral form. Promotion of effective communications among and between members should also be promoted. Effective communications can be achieved through the cooperative learning exercises and provided through instruction. The leader may also foster positive communication by periodically allowing team assessment exercises. The team assessments can help to determine how well the group is functioning and to identify issues in need of improvement; then, the students can together develop actions to address the issues. Typical questions might include "What are we doing well as a team?" and "What areas need to be improved?" These two open-ended questions can be done anonymously by allowing students to write their responses for the teacher to collect. Discussion and development of action plans can then follow (see Figure 1.4).

Also providing adequate recognition and rewards for individual and team members can help maintain a team in the performing stage. Not only are individuals recognized for their personal accomplishments, but team

Directions: Evaluate your team functioning by circling the number on the scale that corresponds to the degree of teamwork (1 = *strongly disagree,* 2 = *disagree,* 3 = *undecided,* 4 = *agree,* 5 = *strongly agree*).

Our team members communicate well with each other.	1	2	3	4	5
People obey the rules of conduct in our classroom.	1	2	3	4	5
We have team exercises that promote collaboration.	1	2	3	4	5
The goals and learning expectations are clear.	1	2	3	4	5
Conflict is managed constructively.	1	2	3	4	5
People listen well to each other.	1	2	3	4	5
Team members are respectful of each other.	1	2	3	4	5
Team members are honest and fair with each other.	1	2	3	4	5
Group decisions are made by consensus.	1	2	3	4	5
Evaluation of performance is good.	1	2	3	4	5

Figure 1.4. Sample Team Assessment

rewards through group exercises can help foster collaboration and cooperation among team members. For example, the teacher may administer small-team competitions based on team projects and assignments. The teacher can give awards out for the team that produces the projects that are the best in categories such as most creative, complex, comprehensive, organized, and research based. The teacher may attempt to have each team win at least one award and then an overall award for best project. This allows all team members to obtain positive reinforcement and recognition.

The concept of team leadership can essentially be characterized by the following formula:

$$\text{Quality effectiveness} = \text{Quality knowledge} + \text{Quality of relationships}$$

The team's quality of effectiveness can be achieved not only through technically learning content but also being able to get along with people. Much like in society and the business world, people need to have technical expertise but also need to be able to get along with other people. A person who has good technical expertise but cannot deal with individuals will most likely produce an environment of conflict and hostility. Likewise, a person who has high relationship abilities in getting along with people but lacks technical expertise will bring a group down. If the educator can build on technical learning of specific content as well as building relationships in the classroom, these skills will be transferable into society and the work world.

EMOTIONAL INTELLIGENCE

Effective leaders have qualities such as intelligence, ability to motivate people, and emotional intelligence. Emotions play a significant part in leading people. Leaders can be very intelligent; however, if they lack the emotional skills to deal with people, they will most likely be ineffective leaders. Goleman (1995) articulates five basic competencies necessary for an emotionally intelligent leader: self-awareness, self-regulation, self-motivation, empathy, and effective relationships. Self-awareness describes the degree to which a leader understands his or her personal feelings (e.g., anger, anxiety, avoidance) and how these feelings affect oneself. If a leader has a high degree of self-awareness, he or she understands what triggers these emotions in himself or herself. The first step in being emotionally intelligent is to understand what sets off one's emotions, so that one can be aware of them. There have been intellectually capable leaders; however, they lack the ability to control their emotions. A typical example is a teacher who fully understands the content but is unable to control his or her anger and fits of rage in dealing with students.

The competency of self-regulation describes the leader's ability to monitor his or her emotional feelings and be able to regulate them. Once feelings are triggered, the leader is then able to employ the necessary skills to control negative behaviors and regulate them in the most productive way. This may be done through self-talk and self-control. For example, if a leader is dealing with students and a student triggers an emotional feeling within the leader, an effective leader is aware of this trigger and is able to self-regulate emotions so that they do not create negative behavior.

Self-motivation is the third competency that describes a leader's ability to direct his or her feelings toward a constructive purpose. All leaders experience successes and failures. When a leader is able to recognize failures and be realistic and is able to grow and learn from mistakes, this suggests competence in this self-motivation level. The leader's ability to discern between important issues and an unimportant issue can be critical in this stage.

The empathy competency is the fourth level that describes a leader's ability to not only recognize and regulate his or her emotions but be able to understand how these emotions affect other people. In this stage the leader is able to see from another person's perspective and be aware of verbal and nonverbal communication. The ability of a leader to give positive feedback and accept constructive criticism is critical in the empathy stage. For example, a leader may obtain feedback from his or her people that can be valuable in learning and growing.

The last level of emotional intelligence is that of effective relationships. Effective leaders who are emotionally intelligent must be able to create inspiring environments, value others, and be willing to mentor and support others. Essentially, at this stage, the leader must be able to separate his or her ego from issues. In this way the leader can be objective in dealing with people. Therefore, the ability to motivate and inspire people requires a leader to be emotionally intelligent and have skills in the five competencies.

POWER AND LEADERSHIP

All leaders have a degree of power. Power is the ability to get what you want. If a teacher desires his or her students to learn, he or she will have different degrees of power and influence in accomplishing the goal based on the amount of power. However, power comes in many different forms, and the belief that a leader must use force in getting a student to learn is a fallacy. Force may be only one method in motivating a student to learn but may not be the most effective. There are five major sources of power, including reward power, coercive power, legitimate power, reverent power, and expert power (French & Bell, 1995).

Reward Power

Reward power is the ability of the leader to provide intrinsic and extrinsic rewards to students. Reward power is used extensively in teaching. Students are highly motivated by many types of rewards, and the ability to provide these rewards appropriately can obtain significant results in learning. The educator's ability to recognize when to use this reward power is critical for teaching. A teacher who does not use this source of power will be less effective in motivating his or her students. Likewise, if a teacher uses this source of power too much, it may become ineffective and rewards will be taken for granted.

Coercive Power

Coercive power is the ability that a leader has to punish or provide negative value to students. This type of power can be effective for a teacher but should not be overused. Most students recognize this type of power and adjust their behavior based on it. For example, coercive power can be particularly useful in helping to maintain order and discipline in the classroom. However, coercive power has limitations in motivating students to perform well. In fact, coercive power may not be suitable for motivating students but rather may provide a mechanism to force a student to a result. For example, the leader may threaten a student with disciplinary measures or negative consequences if a student does not complete an assignment. Although this helps the student toward the result, it may not be motivating the student to personally appreciate the learning. Therefore, the leader must be careful and use coercive power sparingly.

Legitimate Power

Legitimate power is the power that is vested with the leader as a result of the position. For example, the administration gives legitimate power to the teaching position, and, as a result, a certain degree of power comes along with this authority. For example, the mere sanctioning of a leader with the title of teacher allows him or her to exercise authority in managing student behavior. Much like coercive power and reward power, legitimate power should be used appropriately. The overuse of legitimate power can lose its influence. If a teacher needs to exert himself or herself by indicating that he or she has the power vested in the position, he or she may lose respect in the eyes of the students. This legitimate power also allows the teacher as a leader to provide and have control over educational resources. Legitimate power gives the teacher the authority to administer resources and provide an educational setting within the classroom so that students can learn.

Reverent Power

Reverent power is the fourth source of power and is especially useful for a leader to manage students. Reverent power is a tricky source of power to explain and acquire, because it suggests that people have a certain degree of power based on students' attraction to and positive feelings toward the leader. This source of power might be described as the degree of charisma and personality of the leader. Every leader as an individual has a certain degree of strength within his or her own personality. This air of confidence and personal magnetism are characteristics of reverent power. For example, John F. Kennedy, as president, had a high degree of reverent power. He was a president whom many people believed had significant charisma and personality. As a result, many people felt comfortable with him. Therefore, a teacher as a leader needs to recognize the degree of reverent power that he or she possesses, and this can be a major influence in motivating and leading students. Students will be motivated to learn in order to satisfy and please a teacher with this reverent power. The student may be more motivated to perform based on the desire to satisfy the teacher versus the fear of a threat through coercive power or the acquisition of a reward based on reward power. Much of reverent power may be based on the innate personality of the leader. Therefore, the leader may not be able to develop this power within himself or herself. However, the reverent power may be developed through the caring and respect that a leader gives to his or her students.

Expert Power

The last source of power is expert power. Expert power can be described as a leader's possessing expertise or authority of knowledge. A leader who has a high degree of expertise obtains expert power because of his or her knowledge. Students will sometimes respect the leader who is knowledgeable versus the leader whom they perceive as not having much expertise. The lack of expertise may cause the students to be unmotivated. A leader's people skills and expertise for understanding content are two ingredients important in leadership.

PROACTIVE LEADERSHIP

A leader's ability to be proactive versus reactive is critical for all teachers. Proactive leadership suggests the leader's ability to anticipate the needs of students and take initiative in getting results. The reactive leader is one who is content with status quo, does not have the foresight to anticipate student needs, and creates a learning environment that is not vibrant and resourceful. One of the more popular leadership analyses that have been described is based on the work of Covey (1991). Covey suggested that there were eight characteristics of principle-centered leaders: continual learning, service orientation, positive energy, belief in people, balance, adventure, synergism, and self-renewal.

Continual Learning

Proactive leaders need to be continually learning new methods of instruction, developing new ways to discipline students, and keeping current with educational learning materials. The leader who fails to continually learn becomes stagnant, and students can often recognize this problem, and the result is ineffective learning.

Service Orientation

The service-oriented leader is one who recognizes his or her role as a leader in providing needs for others. In the context of being a teacher, educational leaders need to recognize the powerful influence that they have over their students and to view their role as a servant leader to students. The notion of servant leadership is a moral value that entails a disposition of giving and altruism.

Positive Energy

Effective leaders need to be able to motivate and provide enthusiasm. Covey explained that good leaders radiate positive energy. This ability allows the leader to provide charismatic and engaging learning instruction, which often results in the students also acquiring and reciprocating this positive energy. Besides being enthusiastic in presenting lessons, the instructional method of engaging students can support this principle-centered leadership style.

Belief in People

Common to good leaders is the notion that they have belief in their people. The effective teacher believes in their students' ability to learn. This inherent belief can become a self-fulfilling prophecy. If a teacher does not have this belief in his or her students, the motivation of the students will undoubtedly be affected.

Balance

The proactive leader needs to maintain a balanced life. Covey suggested that principle-centered leaders are not "married to their jobs" and that they also enjoy a range of non-work-related experiences. The ability to have a balanced life can inspire the leader to be more well-rounded and less stressed in the classroom. Also, a teacher with a balanced life demonstrates to students a positive role model and can provide good examples for life in society.

Adventure

Covey, in his sixth principle-centered leadership characteristic, identified the leader as viewing life and work as an adventure. The job as a teacher should be seen as a positive challenge and not as a problem. Many teachers have perhaps heard the slogan "It would be a good job if it weren't for the students." This type of attitude can negatively affect the leader's effectiveness. At the core of a good leader is his or her ability to positively view the job as a profession.

Synergism

The concept of synergism is that the whole is greater than the sum of the parts. Covey suggested that the effective leader is one who is able to integrate the many resources of talent and energy found in students and their surroundings in a synergistic way. The sum of the many individual parts contributes to producing a whole product that is greater than the individual parts. For example, the use of cooperative and collaborative learning exercises can be synergistic in the classroom and help to reinforce this leadership characteristic.

Self-Renewal

The last characteristic of Covey's principle-centered leadership involves self-renewal. The effective leader should be concerned with his or her health—mentally, physically, spiritually, and emotionally. The effective leader is one who is concerned with all these aspects and should be responsive in ensuring that the body has healthy maintenance. A leader who develops health problems in any one of these areas will not be effective as a teacher in the classroom. Therefore, recognizing the need for maintaining a healthy body in all these aspects can contribute to the energy needed in teaching students.

The proactive leader is one who should have high moral and ethical characteristics. Especially as a teacher, the leader should exhibit and model moral behavior. Behavior sets the stage and provides the tone for the culture of the classroom. When leaders are unethical, there can be devastating results. Society has seen major corporations experience financial and personal devastation as a result of its leaders' unethical financial decisions. Likewise, when a leader is able to exhibit high moral fabric, the entire culture of the organization can prosper.

The assumption that the leader is serving the needs of others is a key feature of moral and ethical leadership (Sergiovanni, 1990). The concept of moral leadership encourages learning that is based on moral and societal redeeming goals. Sergiovanni stated that

> if supervision is to be moral action, it must respect the moral integrity of the supervisor and the supervised. That is to say, the exchange between the supervisor and the teacher must be trusting, open, and flexible in order to allow both persons to speak from their own sense of integrity and to encourage each person to respect the other's integrity. (p. 56)

The proactive leader is one who encompasses a variety of skills and behaviors. The ability of a leader to develop positive behaviors and skills contributes to the success in educating students in the classroom. Leading students is a challenging job and requires tenacity, hard work, and commitment. However, the rewards can be abundant. Some qualities of effective leaders are as follows:

- *Proactive:* Takes initiative to anticipate needs of students.
- *Ethical and moral:* Maintains high ethics and morality.
- *Self-confident:* Is confident in skills and abilities.
- *Servant oriented:* Serves his or her students.

- *Continual learner:* Continually learns and grows.
- *Honesty and integrity:* Builds trust and respect through truthfulness.
- *Synergistic:* Recognizes that the whole is greater than the parts.
- *Team player:* Is collaborative and cooperative.
- *Motivates people:* Provides intrinsic and extrinsic motivators.
- *Inspirational:* Is enthusiastic and projects care and support.

2

Motivating Students

MOTIVATION AND HUMAN NEEDS

"You can lead a horse to water, but you can't make it drink" is a familiar saying that many leaders can relate to. *Motivation* is a difficult term to define. Essentially, it is the willingness of a person to partake in an endeavor to satisfy a need. Human beings have an innate desire to satisfy basic physiological and psychological needs. The ability to influence students to be motivated to achieve a goal is an overall objective of leaders in education. Oliva and Pawlas (2002) state that

> the first and primary meaning of motivation as related to the process of learning is the disposition or desire of the learner to learn. The second meaning is found in those actions teachers take to arouse a desire on the part of the learner to learn. (p. 153)

Although there are many educational theories regarding motivation, most of them have a common underlying theme regarding the human needs of students. Students' attitudes and behaviors can often be traced to these human needs. Developing and understanding human needs can be valuable in motivating students.

Maslow (1943) articulates one of the first theories on human needs by classifying them into five different levels. The lower-order needs (first two levels) consist of basic physiological needs, including safety and security. The higher-order needs (upper three levels) consist of belonging and social needs, esteem and status, and self-actualization and fulfillment. Maslow's hierarchy can be applied to the motivation of students. Alderfer (1969) modified Maslow's hierarchy by reducing it to three levels: existence, relatedness, and growth (see Figure 2.1).

Maslow's theory and Alderfer's needs models are similar. Alderfer's theory, called the *ERG model*, proposes that people are first interested in satisfying their existence needs (i.e., a combination of physiological and safety needs). Once these lower-order needs are met, a person then strives to meet the relatedness needs (i.e., a combination of social and self-esteem needs). The highest-level need, growth (i.e., a combination of ego and self-actualization), involves a continual desire for learning and developing one's skills and talents to the fullest.

Maslow's and Alderfer's sociological-needs theories have helped educators understand students' motivations and behaviors in the classroom. For example, the lower-level physiological needs (i.e., food, water, sleep, air, and reasonable temperature) are fundamental requirements of life and important for survival. These needs are universal among all human beings but may, however, vary in degree of importance from one person to an-

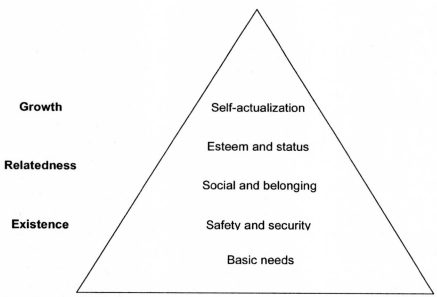

Figure 2.1.   Maslow's Hierarchy as Modified by Alderfer (1969)

other. Students require varying degrees of sleep, which directly affect their behavior and academic performance in the classroom. Some students may have a greater desire for comfortable room temperature than do others for an adequate learning environment. Students who are deprived of these most basic physiological needs may exhibit misbehavior or poor performance in the classroom. Many educators have long understood the importance of meeting basic needs for students. For example, before- and after-school programs have been instituted to help further the academic performance of students. However, educators find that when students are hungry, they have difficulty learning. Parents have long understood the importance of providing a well-balanced diet for their children so that they can sufficiently sustain their energy throughout the day.

A student who has a void in the level of safety and security may also become demotivated if he or she feels that his or her safety or security is being threatened. For example, if the student is in fear of his or her life, he or she may bring a gun to school for protection. Violating school policies may not be important to the student who has a strong need for personal protection. Likewise, when students are transferred to new schools, they may feel uncomfortable and insecure. The feeling of insecurity may be rooted in this basic level of safety and security as defined by Maslow. Another example is the threat of a gang assault, which may be an overriding factor in a student's behavior in school. If the student can be assured that his or her environment is safe, he or she may decide that carrying a gun is unnecessary. Another example of meeting the safety and security needs of students is to ensure that there are safe conditions within the school. If a student is attending a school that has poor structural conditions, the student may feel unsafe. A leader can help to meet the safety needs of students by ensuring that there are proper conditions at the school, providing adequate security (e.g., security officers, video cameras), meting justice and consistent treatment of all students, and giving basic benefits needed to function throughout the school day in a safe manner. If a student finds that there are many students who are reckless and irresponsible, that student may find difficulty in going from one class to another because of his or her safety being jeopardized. Here again, leaders must recognize that the degree of satisfying a need may vary from one person to another. Also, Maslow did not take into account that there may be cultural differences among students.

The social need is one of the more powerful human needs, especially for students. Peer identification is important for adolescent students. The need to belong and have fun with one's peer group can be a driving need that determines a student's motivation in the classroom. For example, if a student's social need is unsatisfied, he or she may resort to apathy, class disruption, goofing around, and attention-seeking behavior to fulfill this need. Another student whose social need is unsatisfied may feel so isolated that he or she may reject the classroom and resent the teacher and fellow students. A teacher who recognizes that a need level such as social need is not being met can be better equipped to deal with various types of student behavior and motivation. There are many things that a teacher can do to help satisfy the social needs of students. For example, a teacher may ensure that there is collaborative interaction among students during instruction. The teacher may also sponsor various social events and school events so that the students feel connected with one another. Administrators can also encourage participation and diversity among students through school activities and structured educational experiences. For example, let's say that one student was actively involved in school and receiving high grades. Unfortunately, her parents moved to another school district, and so the student had to enroll in another school. While attending this new school, the student had a hard time adjusting because she did not have friends and therefore had difficulty being motivated. Consequently, her grades suffered. It is important for leaders to ensure that new students are welcomed to a school. They can help ensure that students get off to a good start and are motivated.

The next level of Maslow's hierarchy is that of esteem and status. Once students feel that they are socially connecting with their peer groups in the classroom, they look to fulfill this next level of need. Students might attempt to fulfill this need by acquiring power and authority. They might also resort to aggressive verbal and physical attacks against other students to gain power and influence them.

The relationship of students' social needs and their classroom behaviors have been recognized by Glasser (1965). Glasser believed that peer recognition is a powerful influence on students in the developmental years. Students have a need to be accepted socially and have a positive self-esteem. For example, once a student's social needs are met, the student will then seek to meet the higher-level needs of self-esteem and status within the classroom. Student might seek attention or might misbehave in order to obtain peer recognition. Teachers should foster a classroom environment that supports the fulfillment of student needs at all these levels. For example, the use of cooperative and collaborative learning may be an approach in which students' social and self-esteem needs can be met.

A good example of a student who is seeking to meet his or her self-esteem and status-need level is a student who believes that grades are important. Some students obtain status because of their high academic performance. Students can be proud of the fact that they are ranked high in their classes. However, a student who believes that he or she cannot obtain high academic success through grades may seek to obtain status and self-esteem through other means. Some students may be motivated to excel in sports, music, arts, and other activities to meet this need. It is important that teachers recognize that the social needs are powerful within young adults and that teachers should try to provide the right vehicles to foster good motivation toward socially acceptable achievements. For example, a teacher can give high praise for good performance, publicly recognize student achievement, and give the student increased responsibility. Students who obtain higher responsibility, such as assisting the teacher in the classroom or acting as a mentor to other students, can reinforce the need level of self-esteem. Another action that teachers can do to promote self-esteem is to give frequent and constructive feedback to students. Giving feedback to students can help them to stay motivated to learn.

Self-actualization is the highest level of need based on Maslow's hierarchy theory. It involves providing educational experiences that allow students to learn and develop their skills and talents to the fullest. Given that higher-level needs are more vague than primary needs, the use of intrinsic motivational factors (e.g., meaningful learning activities, student responsibility, challenging exercises) are probably more effective in motivating students (Kohn, 1993).

Self-actualization is a harder concept for leaders to understand as opposed to the concepts of the lower-level needs. An example of the former might be the expression "Find a job you love, and you'll never have to work the rest of your life." This statement implies that when people seek the highest level of the needs hierarchy, they are seeking activities that they would just as soon be doing regardless of pay. Likewise, the student's love for learning may be the reward all to itself. Some students love to learn, especially if the material is interesting to them. The ability to help provide situations that inspire students to have a love for learning is a common goal for educators. For example, a teacher may provide engaging activities, encourage creativity and innovation, and provide social activities that can foster higher-level learning. A teacher might also take the students on a field trip to inspire them to become interested in a given topic. For example, if some students are interested in medicine, the teacher may take the students on a field trip to a local hospital. If the students are able to watch a surgery or other medical procedure, this may inspire the students to become motivated.

There have been many criticisms of Maslow's hierarchy over the years. Although it provides a good sociological and philosophical framework, many educators have difficulty applying the theory, especially at the higher-level needs. Some theorists have speculated that not all people desire to obtain the higher-level needs of Maslow's hierarchy. If a student believes that his or her physiological, safety, and social needs are being met, he or she may not strive for the higher-level needs of self-esteem and self-actualization. For example, a student who has low self-esteem may have had factors that contributed to this psychological disposition. Therefore, it may be difficult without professional intervention to help a student with a low self-esteem that is negatively affecting his or her learning. Also important is the factor that individuals may seek different amounts of a certain need than others do. Some people simply have a higher need for security than do others. For example, many people feel insecure when living paycheck to paycheck. Some people are greatly affected by not having a savings account, whereas others believe that as long as they are not in debt, everything is fine (i.e., they feel secure). Likewise, students may have different need levels. Some students may simply need more attention than other students do. Therefore, students' desire to fill their human needs in the classroom involve a multiplicity of factors, such as peer group identification, sense of duty, peer rivalry, desire to learn, attitude toward the teacher and school, and a need for attention and affection. However, one thing is common: If these needs are not met, the student's motivation will be affected. Understanding how to meet students' human needs can help students to be motivated in the classroom. Table 2.1 outlines some strategies for motivating students based on human needs.

Table 2.1. **Strategies for Motivating Students Based on Human Needs**

Need Level	*Leader Motivation Strategies*
Self-actualization	Encourage learning for learning sake
	Emphasize love of learning
	Encourage personal learning interests
	Encourage creativity and innovation
Esteem and status	Give positive reinforcement
	Provide public praise and rewards
	Give frequent coaching
	Encourage responsibility
Social and belonging	Provide collaborative learning
	Emphasize teamwork
	Promote interpersonal relations
	Encourage social learning activities
Safety and security	Ensure safe building conditions
	Provide security officers
	Ensure consistent and fair treatment
	Provide safety cameras
Basic needs	Provide food for extended programs
	Emphasize proper sleep at home
	Allow rest breaks
	Ensure proper lighting and temperatures

TWO-FACTOR MOTIVATION THEORY

The two-factor motivation theory proposed by Herzberg (1966) is one of the more prominent theories of human motivation. Although Herzberg worked primarily with industrial companies, his theories can be applied to the educational setting. Herzberg's model is similar to Maslow's hierarchy and provides a basis for understanding human motivation. Herzberg concluded that people experience good or bad feelings based on different types of conditions at work. He theorized that different factors influence motivation based on workers' views toward these motivational factors.

There were two predominant groups in which Herzberg categorized his motivational factors—maintenance factors and motivational factors. Maintenance factors consist of relationships with supervisors, peer relations, quality of supervision, administrative company policies, work conditions, and reward structures. The maintenance factors are also called *extrinsic factors*. Extrinsic factors can be viewed as external types of rewards that can reinforce learning but are not found within learning itself. For example, a student may be motivated to accomplish a learning assignment because of the desire for an extrinsic reward such as candy or a gold star. This extrinsic factor, in essence, is the motivator that is stimulating the student to accomplish the learning goal.

Motivational factors consist of work itself, the possibility of growth and advancement, responsibility, status within the organization, recognition, and achievement. Motivational factors can be considered intrinsic factors. Intrinsic factors are significantly different from extrinsic factors in that the rewards are not tangible. Intrinsic factors, or intangible rewards, are given as a result of learning itself. For example, a student who has a love of music is motivated in his or her music class because of this intrinsic love. In the business world, there are people who are financially successful and able to retire, but they would rather continue working because they obtain fulfillment through their work. Likewise, a student who gains satisfaction from learning will be motivated to continue his or her growth and development.

The two-factor theory of motivation can be applied to students in the classroom. If students' maintenance factors, such as school discipline policies, the administration of the policies, safety and security, and school conditions, are not met at a reasonable level, students can become dissatisfied and demotivated. The lack of clear-cut school policies and the inconsistent administration of the policies can result in students being demotivated. Likewise, if a student believes that the teacher is ineffective or does not provide engaging learning activities, he or she can become demotivated.

As in a company, once maintenance factors have been met—in this case, for students within a school—motivational factors must be provided. These motivational factors, or intrinsic motivators, might include potential for growth and learning, peer recognition, awards and academic achievement, status within the school, and the rewards of future educational opportunities. If motivational factors are not provided, students may never become motivated to grow to higher academic levels.

One of the major drawbacks of Herzberg's two-factor motivation theory is that his work was largely done in industrial settings. Educators have criticized the model as not being directly relevant to education. Herzberg's model nevertheless provides a good framework for understanding motivation. Figure 2.2 illustrates strategies for motivating students based on the two-factor theory.

Low Motivation	Neutral	High Motivation
−1	0	+1

Maintenance Factors	Motivational Factors
Provide extrinsic rewards.	Emphasize love of learning.
Ensure proper conditions.	Provide positive reinforcement.
Give gold stars.	Give verbal praise.
Provide tangible tokens.	Provide advancement.
Ensure good discipline rules.	Give advanced learning activities.
Provide fair grades.	Show appreciation for good work.

Figure 2.2. Strategies Based on Herzberg's Two-Factor Motivation Theory (1966)

EXPECTANCY MOTIVATION MODEL

The expectancy motivational theory is a landmark theory proposed by Vroom (1964) that can be applied to the educational setting (see Figure 2.3). Vroom theorized that human motivation is based on the product of three factors: valence (desire for a reward), expectancy (belief that an effort will result in completion of a task), and instrumentality (the knowledge that a reward will be obtained upon completion of the task).

When applied to the classroom setting, valence can be viewed as a student's preference for receiving a good grade (i.e., a reward). The student may strongly desire a good grade in a class and be highly motivated to perform. However, if a student lacks this desire and is indifferent because of peer pressure or another external factor, he or she has a low valence and is not motivated to achieve and, consequently, lacks the motivation.

Expectancy refers to a student's belief that his or her effort will result in the achievement of a desired task (e.g., successful completion of tests and homework assignments). For example, if a student believes that spending more time on a homework assignment results in a better grade, then the student will spend more time on the homework. However, if the student believes that there is not an important relationship between study time and successful completion of homework, he or she will be less motivated to do so.

Valence × Expectancy × Instrumentality = Motivation

Figure 2.3. Expectancy Motivation Model

Instrumentality relates to a student's belief that a reward can be realistically obtained. For example, the student might believe that the teacher is prejudiced against him or her and that no matter how well the student completes his or her homework, the student will never receive an excellent grade. In this case, the student's instrumentality will be low, and the result will be low student motivation.

Highly motivated students need to have high levels of all three factors—valence, expectancy, and instrumentality. Vroom theorized that the strength of a person's drive to reach a goal is based on the combination of these three factors and that a leader should strive to provide incentives for people. Likewise, the experiences that students obtain in the classroom can directly contribute to their drives for each of these factors. Teachers can help provide these incentives by establishing classroom rules and procedures, fair and consistent evaluation, and proper reward structures.

EQUITY MOTIVATION MODEL

The equity motivation model, first proposed by Adams (1965), suggests that the motivation of people goes beyond just satisfying their needs (see Figure 2.4). This model suggests that there is a direct relationship between how a student behaves and how he or she feels about the teacher's fairness in managing a classroom. Adams theorized that the issue of fairness applies to all types of rewards, whether social, economic, or psychological.

The premise of this model is that people bring inputs into their work (e.g., personal commitment, time, desire, and energy) and expect to receive outcomes (e.g., grades, praise, recognition, and certificates). People analyze the degrees of fairness in receiving their outcomes as compared to the outcomes being received by others. The fairness, or equality, of these factors is subjectively judged by the person. If the person believes that the outcomes (i.e., the rewards) justify his or her degree of input when

Inputs	Outcomes
Work effort	Grades
Learning difficulty	Special rewards
Performance	Psychological

Figure 2.4.   Equity Motivation Model

compared to others, then the person will be motivated. However, if the person believes that his or her outcomes are inadequate or unfair as compared to others, then the person will not be motivated.

For example, if a student is contributing a high input of study time but his or her grade is unsatisfactory as compared to the grades of his or her peers, an imbalance will result in the student's perception. Consequently, the student may contribute less input to learning and more input to other things, such as sports, social activities, or outside work and pastimes.

If students believe that they are overrewarded for their efforts, they may be psychologically prone to discount and place less value on their reward (i.e., their high grades). For example, if a teacher is too lenient in grading, students may ultimately place less value on learning and be more prone to misbehave. A good balance of input and output keeps a student motivated and less likely to be disruptive.

Essentially, the equity motivational theory explains that the motivation of a person is to avoid experiencing negative feelings that result from unjust treatment. These feelings result from the process of social comparison between the student and his or her classmates. It is important to recognize that the reality of rewards may be different from the perception of the rewards. Students often perceive rewards as being higher to other students than to themselves. This is a basic bias that students often have in the classroom, especially when competition for grades is high. The leader should recognize the equity motivation model in motivating students. However, it is not a good idea to show a student's grade to other students. There are often cases where students allegedly thought that other students were rewarded more highly, and the issue of confidentiality then comes into question if the teacher is needing to provide clarification.

MOTIVATION AND SOCIAL LEARNING

Bandura (1977) articulates a social learning theory that can be applied to student motivation. This theory can be helpful to understanding student motivation and behavior in the classroom. Some strategies for motivating students based on the social learning theory include the following:

- Recognize students as team members.
- Incorporate collaborative exercises.

- Encourage social interaction.
- Emphasize social responsibility.
- Promote social accountability.
- Encourage responsiveness.
- Elect students as mentors.
- Establish a peer mediation program.
- Reward students for altruism.
- Praise team efforts.

This theory suggests that people obtain information regarding how well they perform by observing their peer groups. This concept, called *vicarious learning*, essentially means learning through the experiences of others. Bandura suggested that students place greater value on observing the behavior of teachers than on policies and procedures of the school.

For example, if teachers allow rules to be broken, students will mentally process the actions of the misbehaving students and thus misbehave themselves. Likewise, if a student is thinking that other students are demotivated and are paying more attention to outside activities than to learning, the student may act accordingly. In effect, students are constantly observing both their peers within the classroom and their teacher's behavior to ensure that their behavior is consistent with the norms of the classroom. This theory reinforces the importance of reasonable classroom rules, consistency in administration of rules, and reasonable expectation for performance.

Glasser (1990) supports the notion that motivating students through the establishment of suitable class policies and rules is paramount for the learning environment. Glasser emphasized that schools need to pay more attention to providing for the inherent needs of students, such as belonging, power, fun, and freedom. He thought that meeting these needs was essential to creating a healthy classroom learning environment and good classroom management.

For example, students need to feel that they are having fun in class, that they have a high degree of power, and that they are experiencing meaningful activities that allow them a sense of freedom to explore and learn. Glasser believed that the class rules should be consistent with providing an environment that affords the best quality of learning for the students. When rules are broken, the teacher's emphasis should be to establish a quality environment and not power and control. Glasser attempted to re-solve this problem by giving importance to nonpunitive interventions and by refocusing students' attention on quality of work.

A student's lack of motivation may be justified in his or her mind if spe-cific needs are not met. For example, a student may commit acts of im-morality, such as stealing, if their most basic physiological needs of food and shelter are not being met. The student may justify stealing money from another student to satisfy the basic physiological need. Likewise, a student who disrupts the class may be trying to satisfy a social need. Un-derstanding the relationship of these various needs theories relative to classroom behavior and motivation is a key to establishing a productive learning environment.

Another motivational theory that is popular within business organiza-tions is the principle of job enrichment. In using job enrichment, managers give their employees high-level tasks to perform in addition to their nor-mal work. This sense of greater responsibility motivates workers. Because people desire to work effectively, the concept of job enrichment can be useful. The job enrichment model can also be applied to the classroom. If students are given more responsibility, they may be more motivated to learn. For example, if a teacher elects a high-performing student as a lab assistant or mentor for other students, that student may become more mo-tivated. The theory of job enrichment is one that can be considered in the classroom.

MOTIVATION THROUGH NEGOTIATION

A study that I conducted (Tomal, 1997a) examined the various methods that teachers use to manage disciplinary problems. Although this study concentrated on discipline, its theory can be applied to motivating students. In the study, interview sessions were conducted with teachers about their experiences in handling different types of disciplinary problems. Typical teacher responses to questions about classroom disruption and lack of mo-tivation were as follows: "Basically, you have to try and get them to do what you want them to do," "Students play games with you and attempt to get something they want—attention, peer recognition, power, less work," and "Students become bored and demotivated with school, which results in inappropriate classroom behaviors and apathy." Teachers stated that they experience significant and overwhelming stress as a result of disciplinary issues and lack of motivation for learning from their students and that this was a difficult aspect of their work.

The study, which supported the theories of Curwin and Mendler (1980; e.g., discipline with dignity) that healthy environments improve discipline and learning, found that teachers reported that dealing with a few difficult situations created significant stress for the teacher and affected the learning of all students in the classroom. Teachers also reported that, although a few students caused the majority of the disciplinary problems, the teachers needed to manage disciplinary or motivational problems to some degree with all their students.

When teachers were asked questions about student apathy and poor academic performance, typical responses included the following: "Students seem to always want to bargain with you—more time to complete homework, desire to have another chance to perform work," "They often displace blame to others to avoid responsibility," and "They always are giving you some excuse to give them a break." When asked about a student's response to receiving disciplinary action for an offense, several teachers reported that students would plead, "Please give me another chance," or would attempt to receive a reduced or alternate disciplinary action. For example, if a student was not motivated to complete homework and the teacher reprimanded the student, the student would typically ask for another opportunity to complete the assignment.

Teachers also reported that, except for handling egregious student offenses, they did not have strong confidence in the effectiveness of the school disciplinary dean. Many teachers believed that the students eventually came back to their class anyway or that little was actually done to reduce the problem. Therefore, most teachers believed that they were ultimately responsible for managing disciplinary and motivational issues and that they had to be individually responsible for dealing with these problems in their own classrooms.

An analysis of the teachers' responses in this study showed a rather intriguing pattern. The general theme of the disciplinary situations involved a series of interpersonal communications between the teacher and the student, with each person taking a positional view. These interactions between the teacher and student had an obvious negotiation element. In a disciplinary situation, the teacher often took a position (i.e., held a set of perceptions about desired student behavior), and the student took a different position. Both parties (i.e., teacher and student) took positions that were generally incongruent with each other. In essence, both parties wanted something and were engaged in a negotiation process to achieve a desired personal outcome. The party that was more skillful in negotiating its position (i.e., had "street smarts") was often more successful in achieving a desired outcome. For example, if a student had low motivation to perform a learning exercise in a classroom and the teacher was giving a low grade to the student, the student often tried to negotiate a better grade with the teacher.

Many of the motivational or disciplinary situations confronted by teachers were not easily handled in an expeditious manner. A quick corrective statement by a teacher to a student might temporarily resolve an issue in the short term but might create long-term problems by the student's feeling resentment or hostility. These harbored ill feelings may be manifested in student attitudes of lack of motivation or apathy. In other cases, a quick corrective action by a teacher may not always be successful in resolving a student problem. For example, when a teacher reprimanded a student for his or her failure to complete an assignment, the student typically offered a flurry of excuses in an attempt to negotiate a better settlement (i.e., an avoidance of assuming personal responsibility and accepting criticism from the teacher).

Compared to students, many adults resort to the same types of responses in life situations. For example, if an adult is stopped by a police officer for a traffic violation, the adult often tries to negotiate not getting a ticket. Other examples include going through a tax audit, discussing work performance with a boss, negotiating a business contract, or dealing with a legal dispute. In all these situations, adults tend to negotiate to get the most favorable result for themselves. The notion that negotiation is a life process among people and that this process takes place in the classroom between teachers and students is a reasonable assumption. Every day, people engage in interactions with other people in an attempt to come to an agreement on something—similar to motivational and disciplinary actions among teachers and students.

Negotiation tends to be at the heart of dealing with motivational and disciplinary issues of students. Whether or not teachers want to accept the fact that they have to negotiate with their students, they do not really have a choice. As long as people are dealing with people, there will always be a negotiation element.

Regardless of the issues involved, the steps to negotiating in the classroom are similar. This process involves a difference in a position on an issue, bargaining of the issues, and resolution of the issue. The teacher may desire that a student stop talking with other students and work diligently on an exercise, whereas the student may want freedom of talking and avoiding the assignment. The student may bargain with the teacher by stating that he or she is not talking, as an attempt to blame it on someone else in an attempt to win his or her position. The ultimate resolution of an issue occurs based on who, the teacher or student, is more effective in negotiating and whether the teacher exercises legitimate authority.

Motivation by negotiation is similar to the concept of discipline by negotiation and is based on the premise that students, like all human beings, embark on a series of interpersonal interactions throughout the day in an effort to meet some underlying need. Negotiation is a life process, and all people negotiate every day in their lives. Therefore, teachers who are able to develop negotiation skills may be more proficient in motivating their students. Some characteristics of motivation by negotiation include the following:

- Interactions between student and teacher
- Students' having underlying needs
- Bargaining in the classroom
- Students' desiring the best result on issues
- Successful negotiations that motivate students
- Conflict results with opposing views
- Negotiation as a life process

3

Motivating and Incentive Systems

MOTIVATION INCENTIVE STUDY

Motivating students and maintaining discipline have consistently been among the top leading concerns of educators for the past few decades. According to Rose and Gallup (2005), "the question asked in every year since 1969 gives those surveyed the chance to mention the biggest problem the schools in their communities face. Discipline topped the list for the first 16 years of the poll" (p. 49). Motivation and discipline are intricately linked. If a student is misbehaving in class, he or she will not be motivated to learn. Likewise, many disciplinary problems have an underlying cause of lack of motivation (Kohn, 1993). Educators have used a variety of approaches and creative schemes for managing student behavior and improving their motivation. Given this variety of approaches, educators are constantly searching for effective means of motivating their students and maintaining good behavior. The ability of the teacher to effectively motivate students is an essential component for students' academic achievement. Developing a school culture that provides incentives for good motivation may be the foundation for motivational success.

I conducted a study (see Tomal, 1999) to help determine the most effective motivational factors for students. The study was conducted over a period of 9 months. There were 90 elementary and high school public school teachers from several districts in northeast Illinois who participated in the study. Although the districts represented a diverse ethnic background, the majority of the respondents taught in Chicago or suburban Chicago schools.

Data were collected through the use of a questionnaire, group and individual interviews, and limited observations of student–teacher interactions. The questionnaire consisted of a list of intrinsic and extrinsic motivational factors. The participants were asked to rank from 1 to 10 the factors that they believed were most important for motivating their students. Discussion was then held with the participants in a small-group setting (see Figure 3.1). Each of the 10 motivational factors was explained to the participants to have a common understanding of their definitions.

The group interviews were conducted in conjunction with the questionnaire. The questionnaire was used to help provide a foundation for conducting on-site interviews by allowing the teachers to identify a range of motivational factors from which to reference. The interview questions consisted of a series of open-ended questions, such as "What are some of the most difficult aspects in motivating students?" "Describe a typical example of students who are demotivated," and "What are methods that seem to be the most effective in motivating your students?" The group interviews appeared to offer a synergistic element to the session by allowing the participants to discuss and further elaborate upon their opinions. The individual interviews allowed teachers to be self-critical in providing examples of their own inadequacies in handling student motivational problems. There were several limitations to the study, including small sampling group, lack of audio recording of interviews (which could have provided improved documentation of responses), and limited observations of teacher–student

Directions: Rank these factors from 1 to 10 (1 being most important and 10 being least important) that you believe are most important for motivating students.

Good school and classroom conditions	_____
Students feeling socially connected with their peers	_____
Fair discipline by teachers and administrators	_____
Teacher verbal appreciation for good performance	_____
Tangible rewards (stickers, candy, recognition letters, etc.)	_____
Good grades	_____
Teacher giving encouragement to students	_____
Teacher giving regular feedback (e.g., coaching)	_____
Providing engaging instruction and curriculum	_____
Maintaining good classroom management	_____

Figure 3.1.   Student Motivational Survey—High School Teacher

interactions. The numerical data collected from 45 elementary school teachers were analyzed by calculating means, medians, standard deviations, and ranking of the order of importance (see Table 3.1).

The teachers believed that the most important motivational factor for students was that of providing engaging instruction. Teachers provided many comments to support this ranking, such as "If students are engaged in constructive learning activities, they will be motivated." Both discipline and motivation are generally not a problem when students are engaged in challenging learning experiences. Some teachers had difficulty separating engaging instruction from good classroom management. Some teachers believed that although a class of students could be involved in engaging instruction, some may be engaged in the experience but not necessarily in the learning. Examples included students who are having fun in the experiences and social contact with their peers. Most teachers explained that the definition of *engaging instruction* means that students are learning content in an enthusiastic manner.

The second factor that ranked most important for motivating students was that of ensuring good classroom management. Several teachers believed that good classroom management is a prerequisite for providing engaging instruction. However, most teachers thought that by providing engaging instruction, good classroom management would follow. By definition, good classroom management consisted of students following the rules and procedures of the classroom and being respectful to one another.

Table 3.1.   Data Collected From Elementary School Teachers Regarding Most Effective Motivational Factors for Students

Motivational Factors	M	Mdn	SD
Engaging instruction	2.06	2	.90
Good class management	3.71	4	1.95
Teacher giving encouragement	3.91	4	1.80
Teacher giving regular feedback	5.14	5	1.84
Teacher verbal appreciation	5.29	5.5	2.00
Good school/class conditions	6.45	7	2.41
Tangible rewards (stickers, candy)	6.59	8	2.83
Fair discipline by teachers	6.77	7	2.14
Good grades	7.41	9	2.76
Students feel socially connected	7.43	8	1.82

Note: N = 45.

The third motivational factor of importance was that of the teacher giving encouragement to students. There were several teachers who supported this factor through such statements as "I need to constantly be encouraging my students to be motivated and to perform at their highest level." Without encouragement, some students are not motivated to continue to learn.

The fifth motivational factor consisted of verbal appreciation for good performance. This motivational factor was useful, particularly for students who were producing good results or making improvement. Teachers emphasized that can be effective as long as it is not overly used. It also has to be meaningful.

The sixth factor for motivation was that of good school and classroom conditions. Several teachers recognized that if conditions are so poor that students are unable to learn, this would be the most important factor of all. However, most schools have conditions that can support learning, and these conditions may not be as important as some of the other factors (engaging instruction, classroom management).

The seventh motivational factor of importance was that of tangible rewards (stickers, candy, and recognition letters). There were mixed feelings on the use of tangible rewards by these teachers. Some thought that some students were highly motivated to obtain these rewards, but for others the rewards were ineffective. Also, several teachers believed that the overuse of tangible rewards could backfire. The use of tangible rewards can provide motivation for some students but may not be the most effective method (Kohn, 1993).

The eighth motivation factor of importance was that of providing fair discipline by teachers and administrators. Several teachers believed that discipline was important, however, not as important to motivating students as some of the other factors. Several teachers thought that as long as discipline is not administered in extreme fashion, students will not be demotivated. However, if discipline is significantly unfair or there are egregious actions and inconsistencies by teachers in administering discipline, a student could be significantly demotivated.

The ninth motivational factor was that of good grades. Elementary teachers explained that grades are not as important to students of lower grade levels than to those of higher grade levels. One teacher explained that first-grade students are simply not concerned with grades and progress levels and that grades are not even an issue at this class level. However, as students progress through higher grade levels, grades become more important.

The last motivational factor as determined by the elementary school teachers was that of students feeling socially connected with their peers. Teachers believed that at the lower grade levels students are more motivated and connected with the teacher than with their fellow classmates. The teacher's ability to establish a positive relationship to motivate students is critical. However, as students advance to higher grade levels, they have a stronger desire to feel socially connected with their peers. The results of the high school teachers' rankings of the motivational factors are described in Table 3.2.

The high school teachers believed that the most important factor was that of providing engaging instruction to their students. Teachers commented that students have a "short attention span, and the need to provide engaging instruction is critical so that students will not become demotivated or misbehave." The second-most important factor was that of good grades, which was tied with the teacher giving encouragement. Teachers believed that students are motivated to receive good grades, especially, students who plan on attending college. However, good grades were a tie in the rankings with a teacher's giving encouragement to students. Several teachers commented that the need to give encouragement to students provided a motivation for students to continually perform better.

The fourth motivational factor of importance as determined by high school teachers was that of the teachers giving regular feedback (coaching) to their students. At the higher grade levels, teachers believed that

Table 3.2. High School Teachers' Rankings of Motivational Factors

Motivational Factors	M	Mdn	SD
Providing engaging instruction	2.00	2	0.75
Good grades	3.64	3	2.25
Teacher giving encouragement	3.64	3	1.73
Teacher giving regular feedback	5.09	6	1.18
Ensure good class management	5.81	4	3.25
Fair discipline by teachers	6.36	7	1.51
Teacher verbal appreciation	6.45	6	0.80
Tangible rewards (stickers, candy)	7.27	9	2.37
Good school/class conditions	8.20	8	1.64
Students feel socially connected	8.55	9	2.30

Note: $N = 45$.

students appreciated individual coaching and attention that could not be given to students as a group. Individual feedback was critical for fostering a positive relationship as well.

The fifth motivational factor was that of ensuring good class management. Several comments indicated that as long as a positive relationship has been established by a teacher with the students and there is good engaging instruction, class management generally does not become an issue. However, the need to have clear rules and procedures and respect for one another was fundamental for student motivation.

The sixth motivational factor was that of fair discipline by teachers. Several teachers made comments similar to those of the elementary school teachers in that, as long as teachers do not partake in extreme unfairness, the students will not become unmotivated.

The seventh motivation factor was that of teachers' verbal appreciation. Several teachers believed that verbal appreciation is often overused and that it is less effective at the high school level. Some teachers believed that verbal appreciation was critical but should be used sparingly and that, therefore, the other factors were more important on an ongoing basis.

The eighth motivational factor was that of tangible rewards. Several comments supported this motivational factor, suggesting that students appreciate receiving recognition letters and other extrinsic rewards; however, tangible rewards are simply not as important as the other factors.

The ninth motivational factor consists of having good school and class conditions. Supporting comments included that "reasonable environmental and physical conditions must exist for student learning." However, most schools tend to have these conditions as a minimum level, and improving conditions are not as effective as the other factors.

The last motivational factor is that of the students feeling socially connected with their peers. Several teachers commented that being socially connected with their peers is critical for students' social well-being but not necessarily for being motivated to learn. Some teachers thought that when students are too connected with their peers, they may be demotivated because they take learning less seriously, because of their peer influence. Several teachers had mixed feelings on the relationship between motivation and social connection with student peers.

Table 3.3 shows the results of comparing elementary school teachers' and high school teachers' motivational factors. In comparing these two groups, the teachers believed that the most important motivational factor for motivating students is that of providing engaging instruction. High school teachers and elementary school teachers had similar opinions regarding the importance of engaging instruction and that if a teacher is able to provide engaging instruction, then the other factors are not as important. Some of the motivational factors that were significantly different included those of good school and classroom conditions, students feeling socially connected, teachers verbal appreciation for good performance, tangible rewards, and good grades. By comparison, elementary school teachers believed that all these motivational factors were more important, except for the use of good grades. High school teachers significantly ranked good grades as being much more important for motivating students than did elementary school teachers. Several comments supported the argument that older students were more motivated by grades as compared to the younger students because of the desire for entrance into college.

Although there were several limitations to the study, perhaps the most important benefit was the discussion and interaction of the teachers in the group sessions. The teachers were able to discuss with one another some of the important factors for motivating students and reflect on their own use of the motivational factors in motivating their students. Therefore, the sessions were beneficial to the teachers not only in reflecting on some of the motivational factors but in having an opportunity to develop some actions to improve their own teacher effectiveness in motivating students.

Table 3.3. Motivational Factor Comparison for Elementary and High School Teachers

Motivational Factors	Elementary Teachers			High School Teachers		
	M	Mdn	SD	M	Mdn	SD
Good school/class conditions	6.45*	7	2.41	8.20	8	1.64
Students feel socially connected	7.43*	8	1.82	8.55	9	2.30
Fair discipline by teachers	6.77	7	2.14	6.36	7	1.51
Teacher verbal appreciation	5.29*	5.5	2.00	6.45	6	0.80
Tangible rewards (e.g., stickers)	6.59**	8	2.83	7.27	9	2.37
Good grades	7.41*	9	2.76	3.64	3	2.25
Teacher giving encouragement	3.91	4	1.80	3.64	3	1.73
Teacher giving regular feedback	5.14	5	1.84	5.09	6	1.18
Providing engaging instruction	2.06	2	0.90	2.0	2	0.75
Ensure good class management	3.71*	4	1.95	5.81	4	3.25

Note: $N = 45$.
*$p < .01$. **$p < .05$.

Future studies on the benefits of motivational factors may be helpful in providing insight into the use of intrinsic and extrinsic factors for motivating students.

VALUES AND MOTIVATION

One of the bases for understanding student motivation may rest with the fundamental foundation of a student's personal value system. A person's values are determined by such factors as geographical area, religion, school culture, economic status, media, and peer group. Typical values include morality, use of power, loyalty, sense of justice, honesty and trust, and need for achievement. A person's values help determine his or her character. Therefore, values and character are intricately linked. Algozzine and Jazzar (2006) state, "Character education is a broad term that is used to describe the curricula as well as organizational features of schools that inspire the learning of fundamental values by students" (p. 76).

The formation of a student's value system is often determined at an early age and can affect the student's future motivation toward learning, as well as attitude toward school. There are three stages of a person's value system: imprinting, modeling, and socialization.

The imprinting stage begins when the student is an infant. During this stage, the child mimics the behaviors of those around him or her. These learned behaviors are reinforced as the infant develops.

The modeling stage begins around 8 years old and ends during the early teenage years. During modeling, students identify role models and adapt similar attitudes and behaviors. Students at this stage often begin to copy and adopt the styles of their parents, peers, media personalities, and celebrities.

Socialization involves the development of a student's value system based on his or her interaction with other students and people. This stage is formed throughout the teenage years. The idea of the significant other becomes a powerful influence on how well students are motivated in the classroom.

Given their value systems, students may place varying degrees of value on school and, consequently, their degree of motivation for achieving academic performance. A student's value system is often determined by his or her environment—family, peer group, teachers, and neighborhood. For example, if a student grows up in an environment where education is not valued and work is more important, the student may be less motivated to excel in school. If most of the student's role models stress the importance of getting a job and working in a nearby factory, the student may likely be motivated for these same career aspirations. On the other hand, if a student is raised in an environment where people value higher education and the importance of a college degree, the student may be more apt to be motivated to excel in school because of this basic value system. Education may also be viewed as something to endure until the student can enter the working world and make money for survival, whereas another student may view education as a means for achieving financial and quality of life success. Therefore, students may place differing significance on the value of homework, learning and growth, and the investment in educational resources.

It is important for teachers to understand the impact of a student's value system in relationship to student motivation. All students are different, and these individual differences are often based on a student's programmed value system, which affects how he or she learns and is motivated to learn. In-service teacher workshops based on understanding individual differences, values, interpersonal relations, and character education can significantly help teachers better understand the underlying reasons for student attitudes, character, and motivational behaviors. Romanowski (2005) states that "character education must become an integral part of school life. Schools must become communities where virtues such as responsibility, hard work, honesty, and respect are taught, discussed and debated, practiced, expected and celebrated" (p. 23).

PERSONALITY AND MOTIVATION

One model that can be helpful in understanding student motivation and behavior is the life position model (Tomal, 1999). This model was developed based on the theories of transactional analysis and can be useful in helping to understand peoples' personalities and behaviors (Berne, 1964; Harris, 1969). As an outgrowth of transactional analysis, the life position theory provides a foundation for understanding human personality and the possible root causes of student demotivation (see Figure 3.2).

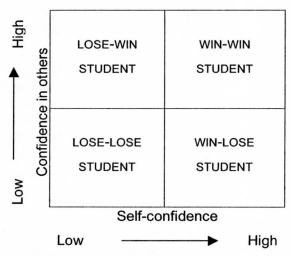

Figure 3.2.   Life Position Model

The premise of the life position theory suggests that the development of a student's personality is largely based on the treatment that he or she received as a child. For example, the first personality, the win-win student, refers to the student who has a healthy disposition about school and life. This student feels good about himself or herself and others. This student readily accepts compliments from others and also gives compliments to other people.

The Win-Win Student

The personality of the win-win student is developed as an outgrowth of his or her being raised in a normal and loving home in which he or she receives appropriate upbringing and respect from his or her parents. As an infant, this child is given love and nurturance and learns to feel good about himself or herself. The win-win student is conditioned to respect authority and, consequently, his or her school, teachers, and classmates. The attitude of the win-win student is one of a cooperative spirit in which there is a positive and open desire to have healthy relationships and be motivated to succeed. The win-win student is generally a motivated person. This student communicates his or her feelings in an acceptable manner. The challenge of the teacher in dealing with win-win students is to continually reinforce their good motivation so that they can remain motivated to perform to their highest potential.

The Win-Lose Student

The second personality, the win-lose student, is the person who fundamentally has a life position that he or she is always right and that everyone else is against him or her. The win-lose student is filled with anger and resentment and is critical about teachers and the school. He or she has high confidence in himself or herself but believes that others do not. The development of this win-lose personality is based on the child's upbringing in a hostile or physical environment. For example, as an infant, the win-lose student might be physically abused by a parent. Given that an infant does not understand the reason for the abuse, the child can understand only how he or she feels as a result of the abuse. This infant develops a position that, when his or her parent is around him or her, he or she feels bad and hurts because of the physical pain inflicted on him or her. As a result, the win-lose student develops a personality that indicates that "if I am by myself, I feel good and I must not be the problem, but when others are around me, I feel bad and hurt, so others must be bad."

This attitude is reinforced by the win-lose child and develops into a personality position for the rest of his or her life. Typical behavior of win-lose students in the classroom is based on an attitude that the school is out to get them and that rules are a form of punishment. The win-lose students are demanding to teachers, enjoy putting others down through their cynical and fault-finding attitude, and are not motivated to learn. They often become involved in gangs and violent activities. In severe cases, the win-lose student may ultimately end up in jail.

Win-lose students are constantly causing problems in the classroom and in society. They refuse to accept any responsibility for their behavior. Win-lose students can be difficult people to manage within the school setting. They harbor a deep-down feeling of low self-esteem but manifest this attitude through seeking power. They often associate with students who have similar attitudes. The win-lose student may attempt to influence vulnerable students and control them. Even as these win-lose students commit various crimes against school and society, they constantly seek recognition, and they believe that they are right and that others are against them.

The Lose-Lose Student

The third personality style is that of the lose-lose student. The lose-lose student is defensive, depressed, stubborn, and has little or no motivation to do anything. As an infant, the lose-lose student might have been a product of an unwanted pregnancy and then abandoned in childhood. The lose-lose child might have lived with various relatives in a variety of homes and never enjoyed permanent residency with a mother and a father. The lose-lose child develops a mentality that life is miserable and empty. The child feels lonely, sad, and unloved. When the lose-lose child is with others, the reality is that the situation often turns out to be just temporary. The lose-lose child soon becomes distrusting and loses confidence in the love of others. In essence, the lose-lose child develops a personality that is somewhat based on a miserable and apathetic position.

The lose-lose student is one who typically sits in a classroom and does nothing and is not motivated to learn anything. This student has little confidence in self or others. This lose-lose student may refuse to do homework, participate in class activities, and show any interest in developing friendships and getting close to other students and teachers. A lose-lose student can be a difficult student to manage in the classroom given the low self-esteem and inclination to be insubordinate. In serious situations, this type of student may participate in self-abuse or commit suicide.

The Lose-Win Student

The fourth personality is the lose-win student. This student generally feels good toward others but deep down may feel badly toward himself or herself. The lose-win student lacks self-confidence and believes that others are better than himself or herself. As an infant, this child might have received inconsistent love and affection from parents. For example, the child might have been a product of a home where the parents were too busy with other things in their lives to give much attention to the child. The child begins to feel badly toward himself or herself and wonders, "What must I do to obtain unconditional love and reinforcement from my parents?" For example, this student may bring home a report card with good grades, but the parents may disregard it or give little positive praise. This lose-win child develops a mentality that he or she is not as good as others and can never seem to live up to the expectations of his or her parents.

The lose-win child often compliments others but may find it difficult to receive compliments. The lose-win student often feels confused, frustrated, and lacks motivation to excel to the fullest potential in the classroom. The student constantly worries about failing and not achieving the expectations of the teacher. This student may think that other students are competent but that he or she lacks the same degree of competence and abilities. Although this student is often a person who is hard to motivate and demands constant positive reinforcement, he or she is generally not as difficult to manage as the lose-lose or win-lose student.

The lose-win student, however, can manifest other behaviors, such as attempting to oversucceed by attempting to climb to the tops of mountains without ever reaching the top. No matter how well the student performs, it can never be good enough. This student may also try hard to participate in student activities and attempt to become popular while possessing feelings of low self-confidence. Underneath the facade, these students are searching to receive the unconditional love from their parents. In extreme situations, these students may become codependent on others and may be easily influenced by peer pressure. These students may attempt to become overachievers in life and may ultimately become frustrated and never totally satisfied with relationships or their accomplishments.

Understanding the life position theory can be useful in dealing with students' motivation in the classroom. By understanding the life position of a student, the teacher can have insight into the reasons for students' motivation and behavior. For example, in dealing with the win-lose student, a teacher may find it important to be stern and assertive. The win-lose student may often become demanding and cynical and attempt to blame others for his or her behavior. The teacher needs to understand that this win-lose student needs to develop responsibility for his or her behavior, and the teacher should not tolerate the student's attempts to blame others.

The lose-lose student can be a difficult person to motivate in the classroom. Many times these students may sit in the classroom and do nothing, and the teacher may be inclined to ignore them. This student needs a constant high degree of encouragement and reinforcement as a person. It is important for the teacher to allow the lose-lose student to feel like a part of the class and develop a sense of security. However, the teacher should be careful not to reinforce the lose-lose attitude. These students may state that they are incapable of performing certain learning activities, and the teacher must be careful not to reinforce this victim-type mentality.

The lose-win student is a person who needs a high degree of self-confidence building. The teacher needs to reinforce positive behavior on a consistent basis. Peer identification is important to these students, as well as the building of this student's self-esteem.

The formation of a student's personality is dependent on his or her self-concept. All students live in a multidimensional environment, whereby they learn to understand themselves and others around them, given their situations. As far back as 400 BC, Socrates developed a basic life premise: "Know thyself." A student's perception of self has a major impact on his or her motivation in the classroom.

Students receive a variety of cues and personal messages from their peers and teachers that reinforce attitudes and behaviors. If students are heavily influenced by the ideal self-concept, they will often be motivated to learn in order to reinforce this image.

Peer perceptions of a student help to shape a student's attitude and motivation in the classroom. For example, if peers' perception of a student is one of success, their impressions may create a self-fulfilling prophecy and the student will be motivated to excel. In essence, the views of the peers become a reality in the mind of the student. Likewise, a student's own self-concept plays an important part in shaping his or her own motivation. For example, a student who has a strong religious foundation and believes that he or she is a righteous individual may be less affected by negative peer influence and will be motivated to learn because of these internal values. Therefore, the importance of developing positive self-concepts in students is critical in establishing a culture of high student motivation.

CREATING SELF-FULFILLING PROPHECIES

The concept of the self-fulfilling prophecy and motivation are interconnected. A self-fulfilling prophecy is the belief in an event that can actually cause it to happen. For example, if stock investors believe that a stock will rise, then they will be motivated to purchase the stock, and the stock will go higher in value. On the other hand, if investors believe that stocks will fall, then they will be reluctant to buy the stock, and they will sell it, thereby causing the value of the stock to go down. Likewise, in education, if a teacher's expectation for a student is high, chances are that the student will be motivated to meet the expectations. In essence, beliefs become reality.

Expectations must be realistic. Placing unrealistic or too high expectations for a student not only can cause a student to fail but can demotivate him or her. Establishing expectations that stretch the student and are obtainable are the ideal aspiration level of the teacher. Establishing expectations can be compared to developing goals. In the business world, it is common for employees to develop what are called *SMART goals*. Good, meaningful goals should be written to the SMART criteria, which are specific, manageable, attainable, realistic, and timely. The SMART criteria can be useful for teachers in establishing expectations for their students (see Figure 3.3).

For example, a teacher should be specific in the expectation to be accomplished; the expectation should be manageable for the student; the expectation should be attainable and realistic; and the expectation should be accomplished within a specific time frame. For example, if a teacher establishes an expectation for a student to be able to complete a homework assignment and learn specific material, the teacher should identify when this expectation is to be met.

Six steps for establishing expectations and creating self-fulfilling prophecies are as follows:

1. Establish a positive relationship.
2. Build trust with the student.
3. Be clear in your expectation (use SMART criteria).
4. Be consistent with all students.
5. Give positive feedback and reinforcement.
6. Provide good follow-up with the student.

S	Expectations should be specific to the student.
M	Expectations should be manageable by the student.
A	Expectations should be attainable by the student.
R	Expectations should be realistic for the student.
T	Expectations should be accomplished within a timely period.

Figure 3.3. SMART Criteria for Teachers

Step 1 involves establishing a positive relationship between teacher and student. This step is the foundation. Without a good relationship, a student may be demotivated and may not desire to excel to his or her fullest potential. The second step involves building trust between teacher and student. Trust is a factor that is established through time in working with the student. Be careful not to undermine the trust relationship, or the student will not be motivated to excel. The third step involves giving clear expectations using the SMART criteria. Without clear communications the student may not understand the fundamental goal in the first place.

Step 4 involves being consistent with all students. Students are keenly aware of the treatment given to their peers. If a teacher is inconsistent in treating one student as compared to another, then the entire group of students may feel undermined and unmotivated.

The fifth step involves giving positive feedback and reinforcement for the student's performance. At this stage the student has generally accomplished work that can be evaluated, and the teacher should be as positive as possible.

The last step involves giving good follow-up with the student. This follow-up may include sending a letter of appreciation or giving additional assignments that reinforce the student's knowledge of the material.

Incorporating the self-fulfilling prophecy within the framework of motivating students can be another tool in the arsenal for achieving success with students. Although students are individuals, unique all to themselves, the theory should still apply to all students.

TAKING ACTION FOR IMPROVEMENT

Learning to provide incentives to motivate students requires an understanding of the basic drives and needs of students, which can be useful in developing circumstances that motivate individuals. Effective motivation requires the use of effective interpersonal relations, negotiation, and leadership skills. Accomplishing goals can be intrinsically enriching for a student. Given that many students desire to be successful, the process of learning can be rewarding for students. The motivation to achieve is similar to the Japanese term called *Kaizen*. This term has been attributed to the widespread belief that the Japanese constantly strive to accomplish improvement. The term is similar to the American drive for success and the need for taking personal responsibility for actions and outcomes. Teachers can provide motivators by establishing high but attainable expectations for their students.

Learning to take action for improvement can be a useful technique for teachers in motivating their students. The ability to set up circumstances whereby all students feel motivated to learn in the classroom is the fundamental goal of teachers. Providing engaging instruction, good classroom management, and intrinsic and extrinsic rewards are just some of the factors that can help. Keeping the lines of communication open between the teacher and students is important to maintaining healthy personal relationships. Students need to feel respected by the teacher and able to talk with the teacher without fear of humiliation. Some teachers may unintentionally communicate in a manner that is insensitive to students, which reduces their motivation to learn. The student may harbor ill feelings of resentment toward the teacher. It is important for the teacher to recognize these pent-up feelings and how they may negatively affect the student's motivation to learn.

For example, if a student is experiencing feelings of anger and frustration, this behavior may be manifested through open defiance. In these cases, teachers need to communicate with the student. The teacher might start by asking the student how he or she feels about the behavior. In this way the teacher might be able to personalize the relationship and draw out the student's reason for the lack of motivation. Sometimes, students use their lack of motivation as a way to get attention from the teacher. The goal of the teacher is to reduce the student's ill feelings to help the student approach learning and feel positive. By confronting the student's feelings, the student is more likely to feel that the teacher cares about him or her as an individual. Dealing with the student's emotions and feelings can also be the first step in de-escalating potential conflict situations and begin the *self-fulfilling prophecy*.

Teachers should not be afraid to partake in concession making with a student. Concession making means giving up (conceding) something to gain something. For example, when dealing with a student who has low self-esteem, the teacher might begin by praising the student for past good behavior or performance. Praising the student during times of conflict is actually making a concession. Rather than confronting a student and escalating a situation, it may be more effective to open up discussion through concessions.

For example, if a student is not feeling confident with his or her performance, building the student's self-esteem can be the first step in motivating the student to improve. Students with low self-esteem need constant praise and personal attention. If the student is not praised for his work, the student is reinforced to have low motivation and ill feelings toward the teacher, which may result in disciplinary problems in the classroom.

Although it is important to use SMART criteria in establishing expectations for students, the teacher should not be hesitant to be flexible. If a student is refusing to do work or is experiencing difficulty, the teacher might need to alter the expectations to keep the student motivated. For example, the teacher might ask the student for suggestions on how a student might complete an assignment, or the teacher may suggest first completing a portion of the assignment to give the student feedback and reestablish expectations for future performance. This method of reducing expectations on how work is completed allows the student to save face, become responsible for the work, and take an active role in working with the teacher.

Every student has different needs, and if a teacher is willing to be flexible, students will ultimately become responsible. A teacher who is viewed as being too rigid and controlling may stifle the students' motivation. This is not to be confused with the need for consistency. Being consistent with all students is important in terms of establishing rules and procedures and managing the classroom. However, when dealing with learning expectations for students, the ability to be flexible and alter expectations is critical given that students have different levels of learning abilities.

Another technique in motivating students is a simple one called the *virtue of patience.* Developing patience can be effective for knowing when to avoid confronting a motivational situation. For example, when a student appears to be demotivated, the teacher might ask the student to step out into the hall or to the back of the room for a few moments as an excuse to give time for the student to contemplate his or her motivation. The teacher needs to be careful not to embarrass or humiliate the student. Although every situation calls for a judgment call on behalf of the teacher, selecting the most appropriate approach and timing can be key to addressing a motivational issue.

Another technique that can be helpful for taking action in motivating students is the concept of paradigms. Simply stated, paradigms are the models that people construct in their mind as to how they see the world. In essence, a paradigm is a pattern. Paradigms are important in how teachers view their students and their jobs. Paradigms can influence a teacher's ability to be creative in using problem-solving strategies. The essence of the paradigm theory lies in a teacher's ability to shift his or her paradigm and see resolution of motivational issues creatively. "It is not what you don't know; it's what you know that ain't so." For example, teachers may tend to deal with all student motivational problems in the same way. Teachers may be quick to jump to conclusions as to the way that motivational problems should be handled. This is often based on the teacher's experience in dealing with students over the years. Therefore, a teacher should not be hesitant about being creative, trying new ways, shifting their paradigms and how they view students' motivation, and being open for employing new techniques and strategies.

LEADERSHIP CAPABILITY MODEL

There have been numerous theories and models on the topic of leadership. One leadership model designed specifically for leaders and their impact on motivation is called the *leadership capability model* (see Figure 3.4). This leadership model illustrates four types of leaders, depending on the degree of the leader's competence and confidence. To understand the model, three terms need to be defined. *Competence* refers to the leader's ability to effectively lead and motivate students. High competence indicates the leader's ability to understand intrinsic and extrinsic motivators and how to effectively use these motivators in motivating his or her students. Competence refers to the leader's effectiveness in understanding and applying the effective qualities of leadership and motivation.

The second term, *confidence*, indicates a leader's feelings of adequacy and self-reliance in leading and motivating students. A leader with high confidence suggests one's having strong spirit, tenacity, courage, and resolution with his or her ability as a leader. A leader who has low confidence is apprehensive, has feelings of self-doubt, and has uncertainty in actually leading and motivating his or her students.

Figure 3.4.   **Leadership Capability Model**

The third term in understanding the model is *self-management*. Self-management refers to the leader's degree of experience, knowledge, and resourcefulness as a leader. Self-management indicates how seasoned the leader is in having a good self-concept and belief in his or her abilities as a leader and motivator of students. Self-management goes beyond only being competent or confident and suggests the quality of experience and fortitude in applying confidence and competence in leadership.

The Incapable Leader

In applying the leadership capability model to leading and motivating students, if a leader has low self-management as well as low competence and confidence, then this leader can be referred to as an *incapable leader*. The incapable leader has the qualities of being neither confident nor competent in his or her ability to lead and motivate students. This leader does not have an understanding of leadership and motivational factors and is ineffective in leading students.

The Obnoxious Leader

A leader who has low self-management but also low competence and a high confidence is referred to as the *obnoxious leader*. This leader, although having high confidence in leading and motivating students, does not have the competence and therefore may demotivate students. This leader is one who is undoubtedly assertive in attempting to lead and motivate students but is ineffective given the lack of knowledge and skills (i.e., competence).

The Timid Leader

The third type of leader is called the *timid leader*. This is a leader who has high competence but lacks confidence in effectively leading and motivating students. Although this leader may have high self-management in terms of understanding effective strategies for leading and motivating students, the leader is ineffective given his or her lack of confidence.

The Capable Leader

The fourth type of leader is the called the *capable leader*. This leader incorporates a high self-management (understands leadership and motivation strategies) and has both high competence and high confidence. This is an effective leader who is able to understand intrinsic and extrinsic motivators and how to effectively apply them in motivating students given his or her high degree of self-assurance. The effectiveness of applying this model rests with the understanding that the term *self-management* refers to a leader's understanding of strategies and techniques for leading and motivating students. Being a capable leader goes well beyond just the understanding of leadership and motivational strategies but also requires the need for high confidence to be an effective leader.

For example, if a teacher has a group of students who are apathetic and consistently misbehave in class, then the possibility of the leader's having both low confidence and competence may exist. This teacher, in essence, may be the incapable leader and needs to develop high self-management abilities in understanding leadership and motivational strategies and the competence in applying these strategies as well as self-assurance. On the other hand, a teacher who is motivated and self-assured to apply strategies but lacks the actual competence still has low self-management because of his or her inability to understand the leadership motivation strategies. However, the teacher who is the timid leader is one who has a class of students who may have problems with good behavior and high motivation. This timid leader may be effective in writing the rules for classroom behavior and in motivation but may have difficulty in actually applying the strategies given his or her low confidence. The capable leader most likely has a class of students who are motivated and well behaved due to his or her ability to communicate rules and procedures of good behavior and motivation, as well as his or her skills to apply these strategies in the classroom.

4

Communicating With Students

MOTIVATING THROUGH EFFECTIVE COMMUNICATIONS

Motivating students requires the use of effective interpersonal communication skills. The ability of the teacher to talk with a student and reach agreement so that both parties feel mutually satisfied is an ideal situation. Establishing quality interpersonal relationships between teacher and student is important for achieving academic success. Wagner and Kegan (2006) state, "This brings us to the third R and the most important element in motivating students to want to achieve as high standards: the quality of *relationships* with their teachers" (p. 42). Basic to establishing a good interpersonal relationship is the need to establish meaningful two-way communications. When people utilize one-way communication, such as when a teacher does all the talking to the student, communication often breaks down. Therefore, the need to provide two-way communication between both parties (i.e., teacher and student) is important in motivating students.

Communication can be viewed as the process of formulating information and encoding this information, transmitting the information to the receiver, decoding the information, and then providing feedback to the original transmitter (see Figure 4.1). Feedback is important because it establishes and determines the quality of communication. This process can occur almost instantaneously on a continual basis between two people.

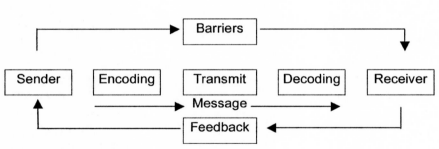

Figure 4.1. Communication Model

Several barriers can affect the quality of communication. For example, the period when a teacher decides to talk to a student (i.e., timing of information), the environment in which the conversation takes place, the personal approach utilized, the method or medium used, and the actual selection of words and content all play an important part in the process.

For example, if a student is emotionally upset and an issue arises in front of the student's peers in the classroom, the teacher should select another time in which to confront the student rather than at that moment. Confronting the situation in this volatile situation may escalate the matter. The teacher may decide that the best time to address the problem with the student might be after class, when they can be alone and the student has had time to calm down.

The environment plays an important part in the communication process. If a student is requested to discuss a motivational problem in a formal office, a higher degree of stress and sense of importance will be established than that when selecting a more neutral location, such as a hallway or cafeteria. If a teacher wants to address a motivation problem on a more informal basis, it may be effective to select a neutral location. The medium that is used (i.e., method of communication), such as whether a teacher uses a letter, one-on-one verbal discussion, telephone, or another person, affects the communication outcome. All these considerations should be taken into account by a teacher in deciding on the best communication approach to use in communicating with students about motivational matters.

Listening is another element of the communication process. Without active listening on the part of both the teacher and the student, the communication process will be hindered. The teacher must ensure that he or she is genuinely listening to the student's position and that the student is listening as well. Most people speak around 150 words per minute, although they are able to listen to 400 to 600 words per minute. With this in mind, a listener's mind tends to wander, and he or she begins to think about other things while listening to a speaker. It is important that both parties pay close attention to each other. For example, the teacher may request a student's full attention before initiating a discussion. Some typical irritating listening habits include the following:

- Interrupting the student
- Never looking at the student
- Pacing back and forth
- Changing what the student says
- Fidgeting with a pencil or paper
- Finishing the student's statements
- Rummaging through papers

- Showing a lack of interest
- Sitting too close to the student
- Postponing answering questions
- Intimidating the student
- Offending the student
- Answering a question with a question
- Taking too many notes

There are many barriers to effective listening, such as not allowing the other person a chance to talk, staring at the other person, continuing to wander off the subject, attempting to finish the other person's sentences, and arguing with every point. Poor listeners also may prejudge other individuals, daydream while listening, become bored, look uninterested, and forget the information in the discussion. Good listeners look for areas of mutual agreement, keep an open mind, listen wholeheartedly, stay awake, and generally process the information that is being communicated.

For example, when a teacher is dealing with a student, it might be easy for the teacher to make preconceived notions about a student, especially if he or she has had problems before. A teacher might prejudge the student and develop a prejudice based on these past experiences. The teacher may not be open to genuinely listening to the student's point of view. The teacher may also have a tendency to abuse his or her authority. It is easier for a teacher to tell a student to be quiet and to lecture to the student than it is to engage in two-way communication. Although it is necessary at times to make a quick command to a student to eliminate a discipline problem, a two-way discussion is essential at other times. Therefore, the ability to discern when to use one-way versus two-way communication is a prerequisite for the teacher in managing a disciplinary matter.

EFFECTIVE NONVERBAL COMMUNICATIONS

The use of nonverbal communication is an important element in discussing a disciplinary matter with a student. Many factors affect nonverbal communication, such as proxemics, kinesics, and effective body language techniques.

Proxemics

Proxemics, which entails the principles and observations in the use of space as an extension of an individual's personality, can place a significant impact in resolving a disciplinary matter between a teacher and a student. Some of the elements that affect proxemics might include the arrangement of furniture, physical distance between teacher and student, size and shape of a room, and physical appearance.

For example, the distance between the teacher and the student can affect the interpersonal relations during the communication process. A distance of more than 4 feet between the student and the teacher indicates an impersonal atmosphere. A personal distance is generally 2 to 4 feet between the two parties. A distance of less than 2 feet might create an intimidating and hostile situation. Although a teacher needs to consider these general proxemic parameters, cultural differences may change the distances.

Kinesics

The use of kinesics involves the study of body movements—postures, facial expressions, and gestures. Teachers who exhibit power may use stern gestures and direct eye contact. A collaborative approach includes a relaxed posture, positive facial expressions, and open body gestures. Although some teachers may think that it is important to exhibit intimidating body language, this may have a negative impact on resolving a disciplinary matter because students may remain silent. The teacher should be aware of exhibiting defensive body language signals, such as darting or glancing side to side, crossing one's arms, or making rigid body motions that can distract the student from discussing the disciplinary problem. Some nonverbal behaviors to avoid when communicating with students include the following:

- Making defensive postures
- Looking tense
- Invading the student's personal space
- Making bad eye contact
- Touching the student
- Crossing your arms
- Pointing your finger at the student
- Steepling with your hands

There are differences in nonverbal communication that exist between people of different cultures. For example, an immigrant may not look a teacher in the eyes when being disciplined. Although the teacher might view the student's downcast eyes as disrespect, this nonverbal gesture may be normal for students from non-American cultures. Recognizing differences in body language in a multicultural classroom is critical for teachers when disciplining students.

EFFECTIVE VERBAL COMMUNICATIONS

There are several communication techniques that can be utilized when talking with a student. For example, a teacher might utilize the technique of *paraphrasing*. Paraphrasing means to repeat back to the student in the teacher's own words what the student said. This helps to reinforce the point that the teacher is listening to the student and ensure that the message was understood. The use of *restatement* is another technique that can be used. Restatement means that the teacher repeats verbatim the student's statement in an effort to encourage the student to continue talking.

The teacher can use the techniques of open-ended and closed-ended questions. Open-ended questions cannot be answered by a simple yes or no and, therefore, encourage the student to continue talking. Open-ended questions usually involve words such as *who*, *what*, *where*, *when*, and *how*. The use of open-ended questions encourages the seeking of additional facts and information. Closed-ended questions can be effectively used when the teacher simply wants to obtain a yes-or-no answer. A simple phrase can yield a great bit of information and expedite the discussion.

Silence can be a powerful technique when talking between two parties. When faced with silence, students will often talk. Using moments of silence in a skillful manner by the teacher can be a valuable tool for opening up discussion and receiving information from the student. Silence can also demonstrate that teachers are generally willing to listen to the student's concern.

The use of *expanders* is a technique of stating simple comments such as "Go on," "I understand," and "I see." Expanders encourage the student to continue talking, and they have a reinforcing effect in establishing a mutual dialogue.

A final technique includes the use of eliminating distractions within the room. A noisy environment hinders effective discussion. Finding a suitable environment is critical to disciplining a student. The following describe typical communication techniques for talking with students:

- Restatement
- Paraphrase
- Silence
- Open-ended questions
- Closed-ended questions
- Reduction/elimination of distractions
- Expanders
- Nonverbals

COMMUNICATION STYLES

An important factor that affects the effectiveness of communication is the dominant communication style of people. Miscommunication between a teacher and a student often occurs when there is a difference in the communication styles. The basis of communication styles was formulated by Carl Jung, a renowned psychoanalyst and student of Sigmund Freud. As an outgrowth of Jung's work on personality, four primary communication styles can be identified—the intuitor, the feeler, the thinker, and the doer.

The Intuitor

Although each of us have and use all four styles, we tend to use one dominant style. The intuitor talks from a conceptual viewpoint and tends to communicate in the time frame of the future. This person places an emphasis on creativity and originality. Intuitors are wordy; they ramble in their thoughts; and they may be unrealistic and dogmatic. They look for unique and novel approaches to solve problems but tend to be unrealistic. When placed in stressful situations, they can be egocentric, condescending, and unorganized.

The Feeler

The feeler communication style values feelings of other people. Feelers are good listeners and observers. To them, the feelings of people can often be more important than the results. They tend to be perceptive, patient, warm, and empathetic. Although they are people oriented, they can be impulsive, moody, overdramatic, and overly emotional. They also tend to operate out of the time frame of the past. Although the communication style of a feeler has many positive attributes, feelers can be overemotional in a discipline situation. If a teacher has a predominant feeler style, he or she may overdramatize a student's problem. Likewise, a student who has a feeling style may more easily break down into tears.

The Thinker

The thinker communication style is objective, rational, and analytical. Thinkers can be effective in organizing thoughts and presenting them in a clear and logical manner. They can, however, be overcautious, rigid, and controlling. They tend to be indecisive in solving problems and prefer to ponder rather than make a quick decision. Thinkers view things with respect to the past, present, and future time frames. Thinkers can come across as being too rigid given their desire to follow a structured, point-by-point format. They may be criticized as being overly detailed, long-winded, legalistic, and too businesslike.

The Doer

The doer communication style is pragmatic and results oriented. Doers act in the time frame of the present. They are hard-driving and assertive. They can be, however, too short-term oriented in their thinking and may lack long-term considerations. They tend to be combative, and they tend to act quickly (and sometimes impulsively). The doer tends to be concerned with the bottom line and communicates curtly and to the point. They are less likely to engage in personal and collaborative discussions with students and are more concerned with railroading their opinions.

The implications of communication styles are critical when dealing with motivational problems. People with similar styles tend to communicate effectively with each other. They tend to talk the language of the other party. However, if both parties overuse their style, conflict can arise. For example, if two doers are talking, they may become too forceful and insensitive to each other. Likewise, two intuitors may become too conceptual and arrogant with each other and avoid confronting the disciplinary issue. The greatest weakness of a teacher in motivating a student is often overusing one's strength (i.e., one's dominant communication style). Table 4.1 outlines some communication styles and recommended approaches to students.

Problems in communication can arise when dealing with students who have a different style than that of the teacher. For example, if a teacher tends to be a doer and is trying to motivate a student who is predominantly a feeler, the teacher may appear to the student as being overly assertive and lacking sensitivity. This situation can be overwhelming for the student, and the student may not listen or respond. The student may view the teacher as intentionally belittling him or her and disregarding him or her as a human being. On the other hand, if the teacher has a thinker communication style and the student has a doer style, conflict may arise. The teacher may be viewed as being too controlling, nitpicky, and impersonal. The student may become frustrated and impatient and simply want to resolve the matter versus having an in-depth and detailed discussion. The teacher may be viewed as one who is too structured and overly cautious and conservative.

Table 4.1.   Commuication Styles and Recommended Approaches With Students

Style	Approach
Intuitor	Be enthusiastic.
	Use whole concepts and stimulating ideas.
	Focus on creativity.
	Brainstorm.
	Allow flexibility.
	Give students space.
	Don't box students into a corner with yes-and-no answers.
	Consider intuition, perceptiveness.
Feeler	Personalize discussion.
	Be concerned with feelings, uniqueness, and individuality.
	Approach ideas in relation to past-proven merits.
	Relate experiences on emotional reactions and empathy.
	Consider expression, teamwork.
	Use cooperation and group projects.
Thinker	Present instruction in an organized and structured manner.
	Give alternatives and do not push for immediate action.
	Be logical and data oriented.
	Order things in a logical fashion.
	Be more analytical and quantitative.
	Consider numbers, facts, systematic inquiry.
	Use problem solving and decision making.
Doer	Get to the point.
	Talk in terms of the bottom line.
	Be practical and concrete.
	Be spirited and down-to-earth.
	Use physical example.
	Consider kinesthetic activities, movement.
	Use goal-oriented tasks.

The key to communicating effectively with a student begins by identifying the teacher's own dominant style, then the style of the student. This does not mean that the teacher must permanently change but, rather, should adapt his or her approach for the student. For example, if the teacher is dealing with a student who is a dominant feeler, the teacher should take extra time to personalize the discussion and be concerned with the student's feelings and emotions.

When approaching an intuitor, the teacher may be dynamic and offer creative and thought-provoking ideas. When dealing with a thinker, the teacher should structure the discussion in an organized and step-by-step approach. The thinker may need more time to contemplate and process the discussion, as compared to the doer, who may be inclined to quickly assess the bottom line. Teachers should get to the point with doers. However, it may be necessary to make sure that the doer understands the details of the discussion when necessary.

Communication styles, like learning styles, can have a dramatic impact on the teacher's ability to improve motivation. Recognizing and utilizing communication styles can be a means to motivate students.

COUNSELING STUDENTS FOR MOTIVATION

The ability to effectively conduct a counseling session with a student is a fundamental requirement of all teachers. Although teachers can at times nip motivational problems in the bud and resolve a matter quickly, quite often the teacher is faced with the need to sit down with the student and discuss the matter. The following is an explanation of the steps in conducting a counseling session.

Step 1: Describe the Expected Behavior

The teacher should begin the session by humanizing the setting and being objective but firm in terms of describing the expected behavior required of all students within the school. Too often, teachers are quick to blame a student for motivational problems without first finding out the reason. By stating the expected behavioral standard, the teacher legitimizes the session.

Step 2: State the Motivational Issue

The teacher should then describe the student's motivational issue in a neutral and firm manner. The teacher should give specific examples and facts to support the allegation. During this step, the teacher should be careful not to belittle or degrade the student and create immediate conflict or friction between teacher and student. Otherwise, communications will be hampered.

Step 3: Ask the Student for the Cause

In this step, the teacher asks the student for the reason or cause of the poor motivation. It is important that the teacher consider possible causes, such as outside influences—peer influence, gangs, home environment, aptitude, attitude, motivation, health, or special conditions that uniquely contribute to the situation (e.g., disability). If the teacher considers these causes, there is a good chance that one of them will be the root of the student's problem. During this step, it is important that the student acknowledge his or her responsibility for his or her actions and identify the cause of his or her behavior. The teacher can help in discussing the cause by offering suggestions. It may be possible that there was no reason (i.e., cause) for the student's poor motivation.

Step 4: Acknowledge Feelings and Paraphrase Remarks

This step involves listening to the student and acknowledging the student's feelings. Whether a teacher agrees with the student or not, it is important that the teacher personalize the situation by at least acknowledging how the student feels. The student might express remorse, anger, or hostility. The teacher can respond by stating, "I can understand how you would feel in a situation like this" or "I can see how someone would have these feelings in a situation like this." Recognizing the student's feelings helps to personalize the conversation and develop an atmosphere of caring and respect. Even for an apparently cold and calculating student, the teacher may still recognize the student's feelings. The teacher should also paraphrase the student's comments to demonstrate that he or she is listening and has understood the message.

Step 5: Ask for a Solution to Resolve Problem

In this step, the teacher should ask the student for a solution to the problem. For example, if the student is failing to complete homework assignments, the teacher may ask the student how he or she will get the work done in the future. Asking the student allows him or her to take responsibility for his or her behavior. During this step, the teacher may need to offer various options, if the student does not. In this way, the student and teacher can negotiate and collaboratively resolve the motivational matter.

Step 6: Agree on a Solution

If the student suggests an appropriate solution to the problem and the teacher agrees, the teacher should give his or her concurrence. When a student suggests a solution to the problem, the student is apt to accept the solution and be responsible, as opposed to when a teacher proposes a solution. If the student's suggestion is unacceptable to the teacher, then further discussion is necessary. If the student is unwilling to consider any reasonable options, the teacher may find it necessary to impose a solution.

Step 7: Explain Future Consequences

This step requires that the teacher explain the consequences for continued poor performance. It is important that once an agreement is made, the student recognize that there will be consequences if the student does not improve.

Step 8: Support the Student and Build His or Her Confidence

This step involves building confidence in the student and reinforcing the teacher's belief in the student. If the teacher supports the student and verbally states this to the student, the student will be apt to improve. Although it may be difficult at times for teachers to state this support, teachers must attempt to restore a positive working relationship. The teacher should also use appropriate body language. The subtle nonverbal cues and signals that a student picks up regarding a teacher's feelings toward a student can be as powerful as spoken words.

Step 9: Thank the Student

The last step consists of thanking the student for attending the session. The teacher should reinforce the positive aspects of the student. After the session the teacher should document the results by writing a summary and filing the information.

IMPROVING YOUR POSITION

There are many methods that a teacher can utilize to improve his or her position. The first is to recognize that the ultimate goal of a teacher is to reach a collaborative solution to a problem that both teacher and student accept. Taking a hard-line approach is not always the best solution.

When an assertive teacher states a command to a student, the student always has a choice of whether to obey. Although a student may obey the command in the short run, the student may harbor significant resentment, which can manifest itself later on. Most of the day-to-day motivational problems can be effectively dealt with by basic common sense. However, it must be realized that in serious situations where the safety of a student is a concern, a teacher must take aggressive action to resolve the matter. Even in serious situations, a negotiating element may be present.

The objective of negotiations is to obtain a collaborative agreement in which both parties are satisfied: They do not feel that the negotiation element is a contest of wills, that they are adversaries, or that the goal of negotiation is to demand concessions and make threats. A teacher can increase his or her effectiveness as a negotiator by employing the basic principles of commitment, collaboration, well-defined expectations, consistent administration, skill development, high priority, high aspiration level, and decisiveness.

Commitment

Teachers must be totally committed to the learning environment to achieve positive motivation in the classroom. Teachers who have a commitment to their students are effective in motivating their students. The teacher who is uncommitted is limited in his or her effectiveness.

Collaboration

Teachers who take a position that the feelings and opinions of students are valued and that negotiation is a two-way street are ultimately effective in developing trust and respect from the student. A collaborative approach in dealing with students can increase the teacher's effectiveness.

Well-Defined Expectations

Nothing can undermine a teacher's effectiveness as much as having ill-defined performance expectations. The expectations should be clear, understandable, and fair for all students.

Consistent Administration

Expectations need to be enforced in a consistent manner. Although extenuating circumstances should always be considered in a student situation, the administration should attempt to be as fair and consistent as possible, so that students will not feel as if there is prejudice and bias.

Skill Development

Teachers who continually develop their skills in managing motivational problems are effective. The values and interests of students are constantly changing, and the ability to deal with students is important. The ability of a teacher to handle different cultures and diverse populations that may have unique motivational problems is critical for the student. Conducting in-service programs and other staff development activities can improve a teacher's effectiveness and skill.

High Priority

Teachers who place motivation as a high priority are effective. Handling motivational problems can mean a great deal of time beyond the classroom. Teachers may need to call parents after school, meet with students, conduct parent sessions, write letters, and so on. The importance of spending time after class hours can lower motivational problems within the classroom.

High Aspiration Level

Teachers who have a high aspiration for student achievement and behavior in the classroom are effective. Teachers who do not place much emphasis on student motivation experience problems. Students are quick to recognize teachers who take discipline as a serious matter versus those who do not.

Decisiveness

Teachers who deal with motivational problems decisively are effective in the classroom. Letting students be apathetic or lazy can only lead to serious problems in a classroom.

5

Motivating by Negotiations

STUDENT TACTICS AND MOTIVATION

Students use many negotiating tactics on a day-to-day basis in the class-room. These negotiating tactics are strategies employed by students in an attempt to bargain for something they want. They negotiate to satisfy an inner need such as safety, peer recognition, power, self-esteem, self-actualization, or other sociological desires.

The use of negotiation tactics in the classroom is an outgrowth of conditioned strategies that students have learned from interactions with people in their homes and social environments. Students learn that to survive in this world, they must develop "street smarts" in negotiating with parents, siblings, peers, and the public. Students bring the use of these tactics into the classroom when interacting with their teachers.

Student tactics fall into three general categories: offensive, defensive, and avoidance. Table 5.1 describes several tactics for each of the general categories.

Offensive tactics are aggressive and attacking-type strategies that students use to bargain a position. Defensive tactics are defending and protecting-type strategies used by students to act in opposition to a teacher's position. Avoidance tactics are denial-type strategies used by students to avoid responsibility for their behavior. Each category has distinct characteristics that students use in bargaining with their teachers, depending on the nature of the motivation situation.

Table 5.1.   **Three Categories of Student Tactics**

Offensive	Emotional tantrum
	Fait accompli
	Good guy–bad guy
	Quick deal
	What if
Defensive	Forbearance
	Projection
	Rationalization
	One more chance
Avoidance	Denial of reality
	Handicap syndrome
	Emotional insulation
	Dumb is smart–smart is dumb

For example, students may use offensive tactics when trying to persuade a teacher to allow the student a special privilege or to take advantage of another student to gain power over him or her. Defensive tactics might be used when a student believes that he or she has been caught in violation of a school rule and attempts to shift the blame to someone else or justify his or her misbehavior. Students might use avoidance tactics to deny responsibility for an offense and to protect themselves from feeling bad.

STUDENT OFFENSIVE TACTICS

The offensive tactics used by students include the emotional tantrum, fait accompli, good guy–bad guy, quick deal, and the what if. Each of these tactics is used by students to aggressively attempt to negotiate an outcome from a teacher.

Emotional Tantrum

Students use the emotional tantrum tactic to draw sympathy and to produce guilt in the teacher. For example, if a student fails to turn in an assignment, the student might respond to the teacher with great emotion by yelling, "You're always picking on me!" "You just have it in for me!" or "You just don't like me!" Students use the emotional tantrum tactic to gain attention by using outlandish and emotional behavior, hoping that the teacher will feel sorry for them and make concessions. Concessions might include a sympathetic response or preferential treatment from the teacher.

Students have learned through their early childhood years at home that the use of emotional tantrums can be an effective means of getting what they want from their parents. Parents are often inclined to acquiesce to their children's demands to stop their tantrums or to reduce their own feelings of guilt that they might experience as a result of the tantrums. Parents may experience personal feelings of guilt because of their desire to motivate their children but not to the extent of driving their children to act out of control. If the parent gives in to the child's demands because of the emotional tantrum, this will have reinforcing consequences, and the child will be conditioned to use this tactic in the future.

An example might include a situation when a child is in a store and wants candy from his or her mother and she refuses to give the child the candy. The child screams and cries until the mother gives in. The mother's intentions are to pacify the child, avoid a public scene, and eradicate her feelings of guilt and stress by compromising her position. The use of this tactic can easily carry over to the classroom. A young female student may create a scene through her emotional crying to her teacher in an attempt to obtain a higher grade. Her teacher may feel sorry for her and feel partially responsible for producing this behavior and may be inclined to accommodate her.

Human beings often can be sympathetic to people who utilize the emotional tantrum tactic. Students have learned the use of this tactic by observing adult role models. It is not uncommon for parents and other public authorities to participate in an emotional tantrum to emphasize a position. For example, children may witness an argument between their parents where the father resorts to hostility to enforce his rules in the home. Children learn that this behavior can be effective for adults and thus mimic the behavior for themselves.

Teacher union representatives may utilize this tactic in bargaining a better contract. Public officials may utilize the emotional tantrum to emphasize a specific position in the media. Movies and television can also dramatize the use of this tactic by showing scenes whereby actors create emotional outbursts to create power positions to win a battle against their opponents.

Fait Accompli

The tactic of fait accompli (or accomplished fact) is used by a student to attempt to bring finality to an issue. For example, the student may make statements such as "This is the best that I can do," "I just don't know any-more," "Sorry, I didn't have enough time to finish the assignment—you'll have to take it the way it is," or "This is my very best effort—I can't do anymore." The student's real motive for making these statements is to ob-tain a final grade and avoid doing any more work. The teacher may be tempted to accept the student's statement as truthful and accommodate the student's request, unless the teacher understands the student's ploy. By us-ing the fait accompli tactic, the student is attempting to manipulate the teacher into giving in to the student's position.

Like the emotional tantrum tactic, the fait accompli tactic is used throughout society. For example, a parent may give his or her child an ul-timatum, such as requiring the child to be in bed at a certain time, but the parent does not enforce the command. The child soon realizes that the par-ent is just using the tactic as a ploy to get the child to bed but that the child can always negotiate extra time.

Retail stores—car dealers, furniture outlets, and entertainment product stores—often use the fait accompli tactic by posting prices on their prod-ucts in an attempt to persuade their customers to pay the listed price even though members of the sales staff are willing to negotiate a lesser price. The wise consumer knows that many items are negotiable and thus does not fall for this tactic.

The fait accompli tactic can be an effective strategy for a student in at-tempting to bluff a teacher. For example, the student may tell his or her teacher that he or she absolutely refuses to complete the homework. The student may be simply testing the teacher to see how far he or she can get away with misbehaving.

Good Guy–Bad Guy

The good guy–bad guy tactic takes at least two students to play. For ex-ample, an abrasive student might begin talking in an obnoxious manner to the teacher, demanding more time for the class to complete an assignment. The student creates a strong emotional and stress reaction in the teacher. After a while, a soft-spoken student follows up the argument by talking in a gentle and relaxed manner, humbly making the same request as the ob-noxious student. The teacher may be prone to give in to the second stu-dent simply because of the manner in which the student behaves. The idea of this tactic is to rough up the teacher emotionally and create tension so that the teacher can end the unpleasant situation by giving into the nice student.

This tactic is an old but very effective tactic when used skillfully. The origination of this tactic might be traced to police work. The good cop–bad cop tactic is used in a situation where one police officer is abrasive and intimidating to a suspect; then, after a while, the good cop takes over and offers the suspect a cup of coffee and talks nicely to him or her. The intention of the good cop is to soften up the suspect and befriend him or her to get information or an admission of guilt from the suspect.

The Quick Deal

The quick deal is a tactic used by students to get something that they want by quickly stating that they are sorry or by attempting to distract the teacher by getting him or her off the subject. For example, the student might say, "Oh, let me run to my locker," "I just need two minutes to finish this homework," or "I won't do the misbehavior again." The teacher may be caught off guard because of the pressure of the situation and may regretfully accommodate the student's request.

Students may use this tactic if they sense that the teacher is distracted or preoccupied with other activities. The tactic can be effective to obtain additional time to complete work or to avoid a serious penalty for misbehavior. For example, if a student fails a test because of his or her lack of motivation to study for it and knows that he or she will receive a failing grade, the student may offer his or her own passing grade to avoid a failing grade from the teacher. Students may intentionally use this tactic even if they know they will get caught. They rationalize their behavior by thinking that it is easier to ask for forgiveness than to ask for permission given that the consequences of their actions are less than the reward.

What If

The what-if tactic is a negotiating ploy that students use to gain power and win a position. For example, students may bargain for a lesser disciplinary action for violating a school policy by offering an alternative course of action. The student might say, "If I behave myself the entire rest of the week, would you let me off this time?" The student is attempting to persuade the teacher by offering what-if suggestions.

Another example is a situation when a student intentionally does not complete an assignment. The student might try to obtain more time to complete it, instead of accept a failing grade on the assignment, by giving a "What if I were to . . ." offer. Knowing that the student will likely fail the assignment, he or she makes a bid to salvage the grade by getting another chance. The what-if tactic can be effective in seeking out information from a teacher regarding the completion of assignments.

The what-if tactic can also be an effective means in negotiating when students arrive late because they are not motivated to wake up early enough. In an attempt to bargain with the teacher, the students may make statements such as "What if I make up the work?" or "What if I complete additional work for extra credit?" It is not uncommon for students to use the what-if tactic in front of the entire class in suggesting to a teacher that an alternative type of test be given instead of a traditional written examination. The what-if tactic can be effective in bargaining with a teacher because this tactic often distracts the teacher from the main issue.

STUDENT DEFENSIVE TACTICS

Students use defensive tactics to defend themselves from criticism by creating defense ploys. Student defensive tactics include the forbearance, projection, rationalization, and the one more chance.

Forbearance

Students use forbearance to make time work to their advantage. For example, a teacher might give the class a deadline to complete an assignment. When the deadline arrives, the teacher may ask a student to turn in the assignment. If the student has not completed the assignment, the student might use the forbearance tactic by stating, "Oh, I'm sorry, I put my assignment in my backpack—I'll have to find it and give it to you later." The teacher may grant the student's request and carry on with collecting the rest of the class's assignments and forget about the student, thereby unintentionally giving him or her more time to finish the assignment. The student is simply buying time, hoping that the teacher will become preoccupied or distracted with other activities.

The use of this tactic can be an effective means in obtaining something that a student desires in the classroom. The student may be absent from school and may attempt to use time to his or her advantage by hoping the teacher may forget about the incident or decrease the seriousness of the incident. Phrases such as "Let bygones be bygones" or "Time heals all wounds" are common phrases of this tactic.

The essence of using forbearance as a tactic is that "patience is a virtue" and that time can be used to one's advantage if effectively utilized. Students have also found that this tactic can be effective in dealing with their peers. For example, a girl may "play hard to get" or put off her boyfriend in an attempt to make herself more desirable to him. People have learned that if time is plentiful, they can create a competitive edge over other parties. People generally do not want to be pressured into something and will create the illusion of having plentiful time in negotiating with another party to obtain a better settlement.

Projection

The use of projection is a tactic used by students to direct, or "project," their feelings or behaviors onto other people. This psychological attempt can be an effective means to distort the facts of an issue. For example, a student might state, "He hit me—I didn't hit him," "She was talking to me—I wasn't talking," or "I'm not being disrespectful—you're being disrespectful." The student attempts to avoid responsibility by displacing the problem onto someone else.

This tactic is commonly used between children at home. Children will often blame each other for their own behavior knowing that it will be one person's word against another's. The use of projection has also been a common technique between parents. A husband might state to his wife that they should go home because she is tired. In reality, he is actually tired, but he is projecting his feelings onto her to compensate for his failure to admit his own feelings. The father may state this in the presence of children, and children eventually learn that this tactic can be an effective means to cover up one's own feelings or perceived inadequacies.

Rationalization

A student uses the rationalization tactic in an attempt to convince the teacher that his or her behavior is rational and thus to justify his or her lack of motivation. A student may use this defense mechanism as a tactic to distract the teacher from the real issue. For example, a student may attempt to justify his or her performance by stating that other teachers accept his or her performance in their classrooms. A typical response may be "Mrs. Smith doesn't care when I do this—why should you?" or "No other teachers have a problem with me." The use of this tactic shifts the attention off the student and onto the teacher and other teachers.

One More Chance

The one-more-chance tactic is a popular strategy that students use in the classroom. Students often attempt to negotiate with teachers by asking for another chance. Typical statements might include "Oh, please let me do the assignment again, and I'll turn it in tomorrow" or "Please give me a break; I promise I'll never do it again." Students often plead their cases by using the one-more-chance tactic, and it can be very effective in persuading teachers.

The student knows that if he or she offers an option for a teacher, the teacher may accept the offer rather than go through all the effort of motivating the student. Students seek to appeal to a teacher's sense of mercy by pleading for another chance.

The one-more-chance tactic is a commonly used tactic in society. Children observe the use of this tactic in the media by watching accused criminals pleading for mercy in front of courtroom judges, or they see their older siblings at home plead to their parents for another chance.

STUDENT AVOIDANCE TACTICS

Student avoidance tactics include denial of reality, handicap syndrome, emotional insulation, and the dumb is smart–smart is dumb. Students can use each of these tactics to avoid taking responsibility or accepting penalties for their behavior.

Denial of Reality

Students often use the denial-of-reality tactic to protect themselves from negative feelings by refusing to admit to their own lack of motivation. This tactic can be used by both high-achieving students or students with low self-esteem. These students use the tactic to protect their egos. High-achieving students may utilize this tactic as a defense mechanism because they do not want to confront the reality of not achieving a desired behavior or standard. Likewise, a student with low self-esteem may condition himself or herself to deny his or her chronic pattern of misbehavior to avoid the associated negative feelings.

Handicap Syndrome

Students use the handicap-syndrome tactic as a method of legitimizing their avoiding responsibility. A student might respond to a teacher through a victim-mentality position by identifying a real or imagined handicap as an excuse to compensate for not performing to a desired expectation. For example, a student might make reference to a legitimate physical or learning disability as an excuse for lack of academic performance. Other excuses might include a dysfunctional home environment, lack of aptitude, or over-involvement in an outside activity (e.g., job, a sport). Typical student excuses for poor behavior and performance include "I can't do this homework—I've got to work every night," "I'm late for school because I wasn't feeling well," or "Come on, give me a break, you know I am dyslexic!"

The handicap syndrome tactic may be used in concession making by the student in an attempt to obtain more time to complete a homework assignment or to perform lesser-quality work. Students who resort to using this tactic may have learned its effectiveness from their experiences at home. For example, a child who has a father with a bad back may see the father use this condition as his excuse for not going to work. Although the father's back pain is a legitimate problem, the father is embellishing the condition to avoid being responsible and as an excuse for his laziness.

A student might use this same tactic to compensate for his or her fear of failure of an assignment. To prevent embarrassment in front of his or her classmates if the student does not complete the assignment, he or she may blame it on a disability. Students understand that this tactic can be effective because it creates doubt in the teacher's mind as to the legitimacy of the student's excuse.

Emotional Insulation

The emotional insulation tactic is used by students to withdraw into passivity to protect themselves from inner painful feelings. In essence, the student shuts down and refuses to deal with the reality of the situation. This tactic can be effective as an extreme technique of behavior, given that the tactic portrays a student who is entirely insubordinate and has completely lost all motivation.

For example, a student might use this tactic to send a signal to the teacher that the student is willing to go to any extreme, such as receiving a failing grade or being kicked out of the class, in an effort to gain concessions from the teacher. The student may also use this tactic to create feelings of compassion in the teacher. The teacher may feel sorry for the student and shift the focus to comforting the student rather than on addressing the lack of motivation. The student, by using this tactic, is able to effectively defer the teacher's attention off the motivational issue and onto the student's emotional condition.

Dumb Is Smart–Smart Is Dumb

Students might use the dumb is smart–smart is dumb tactic by acting innocent, naive, or ignorant about the rules and policies of the school in an attempt to avoid a penalty for their lack of motivation. For example, the student might violate a school policy and then plea-bargain with the teacher by indicating that he or she did not know about the school policy or that the teacher never informed him or her about the policy. If a student fails to do an assignment, he or she may state that he or she did not hear the teacher give the assignment, or he or she did not understand it.

The student uses this tactic to distract the teacher from the real issue and thereby avoid responsibility. Students have observed this tactic being used in the media. For example, many years ago a popular television show entitled *Columbo* featured the main character as a bumbling investigator who was able to obtain a great deal of information by pretending to be dumb. Columbo was able to obtain information because he was able to persuade people to assume a helping role and freely give information.

Students who have exceptional acting abilities can utilize this tactic effectively in pleading their cases to a teacher. For example, a student may be in the classroom and lack the motivation to complete an assignment. The student may use the dumb is smart–smart is dumb tactic by stating to the teacher that he or she does not understand the problem, in hopes that the teacher will do the problem for him or her.

6

Motivating by Teacher Countertactics

TEACHER COUNTERTACTICS

When teachers are confronted with their students' tactics, they are forced to rely on their own arsenal of countertactics. Countertactics are the teacher's weapons of defense to bargain with students in reaching settlements on issues. In essence, the student is attempting to get something that he or she wants, and the teacher, in turn, attempts to obtain his or her own desires.

Although teachers tend to naturally develop countertactics when faced with the various tactics of students, having an understanding of countertactics and developing skills in using them can be effective in motivating students. The key is to be able to recognize the tactic being used by the student, select the most effective countertactic, and then be able to reach a collaborative settlement with the student.

Three categories of countertactics coincide with the student: offensive, defensive, and avoidance. These countertactics incorporate various strategies in bargaining with students, as illustrated in Figure 6.1.

TEACHER OFFENSIVE COUNTERTACTICS

Teacher offensive countertactics are used in response to the emotional tantrum, fait accompli, good guy–bad guy, quick deal, and what if student tactics. These countertactics can be used to bargain with students who use aggressive tactics.

Student Offensive Tactics	*Teacher Countertactics*
Emotional tantrum	Ignore tactic, confront emotionalism, focus on facts
Fait accompli	Escalate expectation, use what-if tactics
Good guy–bad guy	Use fait accompli tactic, change to different subject
Quick deal	Avoidance, forbearance, or confront the tactic
What if	Use what-if tactic, ignore it, or fait accompli

Student Defensive Tactics	*Teacher Countertactics*
Forbearance	Use conditional response or what-if tactic
Projection	Refer to counselor or third-party mediation
Rationalization	Use fait accompli, positive reinforcement, or counseling
One more chance	Use forbearance, ignore tactic, or confront the behavior/tactic

Student Avoidance Tactics	*Teacher Countertactics*
Denial of reality	Refer to counseling, use forbearance tactic
Handicap syndrome	Ignore tactic, use positive reinforcement, or what if
Emotional insulation	Positive reinforcement, use what-if tactic, parent conference, or counseling
Dumb is smart–smart is dumb	Confront behavior/tactic, avoid giving into the tactic, counseling

Figure 6.1. Teacher Negotiating Countertactics

Emotional Tantrum

When teachers are confronted with the tactic of the emotional tantrum, they can feel a number of different emotional reactions. The teachers may feel guilt, sympathy, emotional rage, or resentment toward the student. The emotional tantrum can create an unpleasant situation if done in a classroom setting. Not only does the behavior affect the student and teacher, but the entire class is affected by the time being wasted during the incident.

The teacher can utilize a number of countertactics when confronted with the emotional tantrum, such as ignoring the tantrum, sticking to the facts of the situation, not allowing the behavior to produce an emotional reaction in the teacher, or confronting the validity of the statement. The teacher might also confront the unacceptable behavior and privately address the behavior with the student.

For example, if the student displays an emotional tantrum, the teacher can simply counter with the tactic of forbearance. Forbearance can be used to give the teacher time to deal with the student's behavior by simply asking the student to stay calm, with the promise of privately discussing the matter at a later time. The use of forbearance allows the teacher to defer confronting the matter to a later time so that the incident does not escalate into a more serious situation.

When dealing with the emotional tantrum, it is important for the teacher to focus on the facts of the situation and not become sidetracked by participating in an emotional exchange with the student. The beginning teacher might be tempted to engage in an emotional discussion with a student, which can get out of control. The beginning teacher may also experience an overwhelming sense of guilt by feeling that he or she might have contributed to the student's behavior.

Many teachers, given that they have high concern for their students as human beings, may opt to feel some sense of responsibility for the student's behavior and may want to apologize and try to accommodate the student's needs. A common reaction may be for the teacher to embark on concession making by giving in to some of the demands of the student in an effort to compromise for the teacher's own personal feelings of guilt. Teachers need to be careful not to fall into this trap of letting the student's tactic produce the natural human feelings of wanting to nurture the student.

A student might use the emotional tantrum, for example, in an attempt to obtain an extra day to turn in an assignment. The teacher's quick and easy response might be to accommodate the student. However, this temptation should be avoided; otherwise, the teacher will reinforce the use of this tactic, and students will continue to use this tactic to take advantage of the teacher.

Fait Accompli

When a student uses the fait accompli (accomplished fact) tactic, he or she is attempting to bring finality to an issue. For example, a student may make the statement "This is the best I can do," in an attempt to justify his or her poor behavior or performance. Although the teacher may be tempted to use the emotional tantrum in reaction to the student's excuses, it is more appropriate to ignore the tactic and maintain an adult position.

Good Guy–Bad Guy

The good guy–bad guy tactic takes at least two students to play. For example, if an entire class is confronting a teacher for reduced homework, a boisterous and disruptive student might make demands and purposely create emotional tension in the teacher. After a while, a soft-spoken student may intervene on behalf of the student and bargain for the same, reduced homework, hoping the teacher will soften and concede.

In this situation, the teacher has many countertactics available. The teacher may counter this tactic by recognizing what is happening, resisting the tendency to give in, or resorting to the tactic of fait accompli. The use of fait accompli can bring closure to the situation by stating to the students that the issue is nonnegotiable. The teacher at this point can move on to another topic.

It is important that teachers use the appropriate countertactic for a given student tactic. For example, if a teacher were to use a what-if tactic to counter a good guy–bad guy tactic, the entire negotiation session might escalate out of control. The what-if tactic could not only incite a long discussion on various options but allow the students to obtain control over the situation.

It is not prudent to always use the same countertactic for a good guy–bad guy tactic. For example, if the teacher uses the fait accompli tactic every time, the teacher may be adopting a dictatorial setting in the class, which can stifle the free expression and learning of the students. Using different countertactics can be productive in maintaining balance and a collaborative classroom environment.

Quick Deal

When a teacher is faced with the quick-deal tactic, it is important that the teacher quickly recognize that negotiating in this situation can often produce extreme outcomes. For example, if a student states that he or she wants to quickly run to the locker, and the teacher concedes, he or she may be viewed as giving preferential treatment or being inconsistent in classroom management. The teacher needs to be careful about creating negative impressions for the entire class. Also, although allowing a student to run to his or her locker may appear an innocent request, the student may have other intentions in mind.

When faced with the quick deal, the teacher has to make a judgment call. The teacher should resist the tendency to give in to the quick deal, but should instead make use of the forbearance tactic. For example, the teacher might ask the student to go to the locker after class. Alternatively, the teacher might confront the tactic by talking with the student or requesting that the student become more organized. Often, if the teacher further explores the student's motives behind the use of the quick deal, the teacher may soon discover insightful information.

What If

The what-if tactic is a common strategy used by students but can be easily countered by the teacher. For example, if the student intentionally does not complete an assignment, the student might try to obtain more time to complete it instead of accepting a failing grade. The teacher might counter this tactic by ignoring the statement, suggesting a teacher–parent conference, or requesting that the student do additional work. In essence, the teacher counters the what-if tactic with his or her own what-if tactic.

Other options in countering the what-if tactic include the teacher's stating, "What if next time you complete your assignment on time and receive a better grade?" The what-if tactic as used by the student can be annoying to the teacher, and the teacher must be careful not to become distracted or irritated with the student, which may only escalate the problem.

If the student states that this is the best that he or she can do, the teacher may respond by stating, "What if I were to give you an extra day to complete the assignment more thoroughly?" By responding with this counter-tactic, the teacher allows the student to continue to complete the assignment and improve on his or her performance. Although the teacher may in fact be accommodating the student, the teacher will be able to allow the student to save face and improve his or her learning. In essence, the teacher gives the student another chance by offering a choice to the student with the hope that the student will continue learning rather than give up. The teacher could confront the student using the fait accompli tactic by indicating that he or she understands the tactic being used and that it is being used as an excuse for justifying the student's inappropriate behavior. The teacher may also confront the student to request that the tactic not be used anymore as a ploy and to encourage the student to be up-front with his or her intentions.

TEACHER DEFENSIVE COUNTERTACTICS

The teacher defensive countertactics are used in response to the forbearance, projection, rationalization, and one more chance student tactics. Defensive tactics contain an element of manipulation in that the students are denying responsibility for their behavior.

Forbearance

Given that the basic premise of the forbearance tactic is to allow the student to obtain more time, recognizing the use of this tactic is foremost in countering it. If a teacher is able to quickly recognize the use of this tactic, he or she will not be caught off guard, and he or she will be more effective in negotiating with the student.

When a student uses this tactic, it may be difficult for the teacher to discern whether the student is sincere or is using this excuse as a genuine tactic. For example, if a student does not have his or her homework when asked by the teacher and the student responds, "It's somewhere in my backpack—give me a few moments and I can find it," the student may be simply buying time, hoping the teacher might be distracted and then forget about the request. The use of this tactic can be effective when classroom activities are abundant and the teacher can be easily distracted by other activities within the room. A countertactic by the teacher might include a condition on the request, such as "If you don't find the homework, make sure you stay after class and talk to me." This might be an effective approach in determining whether the student's excuse is real. The student might opt to quickly respond, "No, that's okay, let's forget it," as opposed to the obvious, needing to stay after class. In essence, the teacher has countered with the fait accompli tactic, which brings the situation to closure.

Another example where the forbearance tactic is used by students is when a student bargains for more time when taking a test. Students often use this tactic in an attempt to postpone the test because of their lack of motivation to study. The best response by the teacher may simply be to recognize that the tactic is being used and not give in.

Projection

The projection tactic, when utilized by a student, can be one of the more difficult tactics for a teacher to counter. Given that this tactic has a psychological underpinning, the student attempts to relate, or project, his or her feelings to another person to compensate for the student's own dysfunction.

For example, if a student fails to understand a lesson, he or she might respond by stating, "It's not me; it is because you are a bad teacher."This can obviously be a difficult situation for the teacher. A countertactic might include a counseling session. In the counseling session, the teacher and a disciplinary administrator might be able to sort through the situation to obtain the facts. A student who utilizes the projection tactic may routinely use it as a form of denial. In situations where the use of this tactic is clear, the teacher might use a countertactic such as third-party intervention (i.e., school psychologist).

Rationalization

The rationalization tactic is a common tactic used by students in attempting to defend their poor motivation. A teacher may counter this tactic by using fait accompli. For example, the teacher might state that the student's rationalization is unacceptable and that the student must take responsibility for his or her behavior. The use of fait accompli takes a zero-tolerance approach in dealing with the tactic.

A teacher can also use the what-if tactic to counter the rationalization tactic. The teacher might respond to a student who is rationalizing his or her behavior by stating, "What if I were to talk to the other teachers regarding this matter?" or "What if I were to give everyone a break?"

One More Chance

The one-more-chance tactic is commonly used by students to negotiate another opportunity to correct their behavior. Common expressions include "Oh, please give me a break" or "I promise I'll never do it again." Even though this basic tactic is obvious, teachers may have a tendency to give in to student demands. Teachers can utilize a number of countertactics, such as being obstinate, ignoring the student, terminating the discussion, or confronting the student. The teacher may respond to the student by indicating that if he or she were to give the student another chance, then he or she would have to give all students another chance, and consistency is important. In essence, the teacher is countering the tactic by being obstinate and not giving in to the student's demands.

The one-more-chance tactic can be difficult to counter because the teacher's natural inclination is to help students; and when the student is personalizing his or her request by pleading for mercy, it is tempting for a teacher to give in. Giving in to this tactic can have reinforcing consequences. Once a teacher starts giving in to this tactic, the student may continue to use it as an excuse for his or her poor academic performance. The teacher must be able to separate the true issues of the student's request versus the tactic that is being utilized.

At times, it may be necessary for a teacher to develop a compromise with the student, but the teacher should resist the student's use of a tactic as a means of concession. In other words, when the teacher negotiates with a student, he or she must deal with the issue (i.e., misbehavior) with the student and avoid the tactic that is being utilized. The teacher may confront the student by requesting that the discussion stay focused on the issues as opposed to the tactic being used. The tactic may be a mere distraction to avoid discussing the underlying causes for the unacceptable behavior.

TEACHER AVOIDANCE COUNTERTACTICS

Denial of Reality

Students use the denial-of-reality tactic to avoid taking responsibility for their own behavior. The teacher can use the forbearance countertactic because the teacher may want to wait and deal with the situation later if the denial is being made in front of the student's peers. Talking with the student privately may resolve the matter more appropriately, without embarrassment to the student. Confronting a student in front of the class can only intensify the problem and create resentment in the student toward the teacher. Sending the student to the school psychologist or counselor may be another alternative for the teacher if the student uses this tactic on a chronic basis.

Handicap Syndrome

The handicap syndrome tactic is a common strategy used by students to justify their poor performance. When encountering this tactic, the teacher needs to carefully analyze the situation and determine whether the student's excuse is justified. If the teacher concludes that there is no real justification for the excuse, then the teacher can respond with a number of countertactics.

For example, if the student is stating that he or she cannot thoroughly complete an assignment because of his or her lack of ability, the teacher can counter this tactic by taking an obstinate position and not agreeing with the student. The teacher might also ignore the student's excuse and continue talking as if he or she did not hear it.

The teacher can counter the handicap syndrome tactic by using the what-if tactic. The what-if tactic can be an effective means of bargaining by offering the student other options in getting the work done. For example, the teacher may offer that student the choice to work with other students cooperatively, spend more time with the teacher, or use supplemental resources.

Students who have legitimate disabilities may be prone to utilize this tactic as an excuse for their unacceptable behavior. It is not uncommon for a student with a legitimate problem to use it as an excuse for his or her lack of motivation to perform schoolwork, or for his or her indifference to good behavior. Although the teacher needs to recognize a student's legitimate problem, the teacher must not fall victim to the student's use of the legitimate problem as a negotiating ploy.

The teacher might also try the use of praise and reinforcement by recognizing the positive behaviors of the student. Determining this situation may be difficult to sort out for the teacher, and it requires a careful balance with each unique incident.

Giving in to a student's demand can have reinforcing consequences. The student may use this excuse every time that he or she has difficulty with a problem or wants to compensate for his or her behavior. Use of this type of tactic reinforces a victim-type mentality in the student. The teacher needs to avoid reinforcing this victim mentality and should ignore the behavior. The teacher should also be careful not to confront the legitimate concern and belittle the student.

Emotional Insulation

The emotional insulation tactic can be difficult for a teacher to counter. When a student shuts down and becomes obstinate, the teacher can easily become frustrated trying to open up discussions. The teacher can counter this tactic with use of the what-if tactic. The teacher might respond with a comment such as "What if I were to spend extra time with you and the situation?" In this way the teacher might begin to reestablish communication. The teacher may be forced to salvage the situation by allowing the student to save face, rather than allow the student to shut down.

The teacher may need to focus on the student's self-esteem and provide extra attention and reinforcement as a way for the student to deal with his or her emotional insulation. The teacher may try using praise and reinforcement in recognizing the student's positive qualities as a way to reestablish rapport with the student.

Using this tactic may also indicate deep-rooted psychological problems in the student, and the teacher may want to refer the student to the school psychologist. A student who shuts down with a teacher may also have outside personal problems that the teacher may need to discuss with the student.

Dumb Is Smart–Smart Is Dumb

The dumb is smart–smart is dumb tactic is often used by students to justify their lack of motivation with an excuse so that they can avoid taking responsibility for their behavior. Students may say that they did not understand an assignment. This tactic is used to distract the teacher from the real issue and avoid responsibility. The teacher might counter this tactic by ignoring it. The teacher could validate his or her position by giving proof that the student knew of the assignment.

If, for example, the student uses this tactic in an attempt to get the teacher to complete his or her assignment, the teacher should not fall into this trap but recognize the tactic that is being used to manipulate the teacher. The teacher should avoid confronting the tactic and getting pulled into a never-ending discussion with the student. The teacher needs to recognize the tactic and counter it quickly by sticking to the facts of the incident.

The use of countertactics by teachers is inevitable. Recognizing a given tactic when presented by a student can be useful for a teacher in selecting the most appropriate countertactic to resolve the matter. Experienced teachers may learn the use of countertactics naturally over a period of time. However, learning to better recognize the various student tactics and developing skills in negotiations can assist the teacher in managing motivational problems.

TEACHER MOTIVATIONAL STYLES

When teachers manage motivational problems in the classroom, they develop a style. Much like the administrator who develops a defined leadership and conflict management style (Blake & Mouton, 1969; Kilmann & Thomas, 1977), teachers handle student motivational problems with different styles (Tomal, 1997b). These styles are based on the degree of the teacher's enforcing of rules and supporting of students (see Figure 6.2).

The *enforcing* term is defined as the degree of assertiveness that a teacher uses in motivating students. A teacher who has high enforcing attributes places a high value on asserting his or her position. Likewise, a teacher who has a low concern for enforcing places little emphasis on asserting his or her own position.

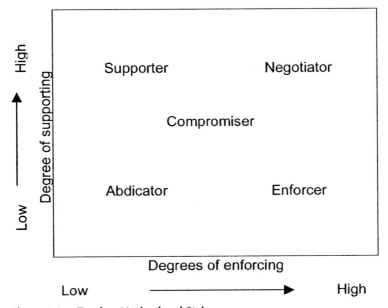

Figure 6.2.   Teacher Motivational Styles

The *supporting* term is defined as the degree to which a teacher accommodates the student. A teacher who has high supporting attributes places high value on accommodating the student. The teacher with low supporting attributes places little value on accommodating the student.

Based on the combination of the enforcing and supporting attributes, a teacher's style can be categorized into five primary styles—enforcer, supporter, abdicator, compromiser, and negotiator. Characteristics of these motivational styles are listed in Figure 6.3.

The Enforcer

If a teacher has a high degree of enforcing and a low degree of supporting, the teacher's style can be called the *enforcer*. This teacher is much like a dictator in demanding that his or her students be motivated to learn, while allowing little room for discussion. The enforcer's attitude is "It is my way or the highway!" This style is directive and assertive.

Enforcer

Self-righteous	Threatening
Intimidating	Demeaning
Controlling	Dictatorial

Abdicator

Does nothing	Ignores students
Avoids problems	Bottled up
Reclusive	Apathetic

Compromiser

Manipulative	Limits creativity
Inconsistent	Gives and takes
Wishy-washy	Open-ended

Supporter

Seeks harmony	Evasive
Helpful, gracious	Personal
Indecisive	Unassertive

Negotiator

Seeks resolution	Responsible
Win-win approach	Committed
Objective	Collaborates

Figure 6.3. Characteristic of Teacher Motivational Styles

The enforcer takes a zero-tolerance approach to motivational problems. The enforcer style is characteristic of teachers who take a hard-line approach with their students and give little leeway to them. They make comments like "The students know the rules of the class, and if they are not motivated to work, they know the consequences" and "I run a tight ship in my classroom." Dictator-style teachers appear to have little regard for individual circumstances—"If I give one student a break, then I have to give all students a break."

Enforcers like to subscribe to being consistent and impersonal. They believe that the classroom should show little tolerance for lack of motivation. The enforcer places a high value on motivation and has little regard for the individual student's personal problems. This style has characteristics of being autocratic, self-righteous, overthreatening, intimidating, and demeaning.

For example, if a student fails to bring an assignment to school but has a good excuse, this type of teacher would not accept any excuses and would give little time for listening to the student. Students soon learn that there is little flexibility in expected behavior, and they may develop a high degree of fear and disrespect toward the teacher. The negative consequences for this type of style can vary. Students may become "yes" students to tolerate the threatening style. Also, students may find it difficult to become personable with this type of teacher and will feel that the classroom is somewhat like a prison.

The enforcer is one who imposes strict rules and creates a confining and controlling climate within the classroom. Students may feel bottled up and may not achieve as well because of their fear of asking questions of the teacher or their classmates. Moreover, a student may feel belittled or ridiculed by the enforcer to the point where the student may seek revenge. Students seek revenge by not coming to class, having a poor attitude, doing as little as possible, or doing something destructive to the school building.

Students can also feel that this type of teacher is unfair to them and can develop a great deal of stress and anxiety by being in the classroom. This anxiety can manifest itself through a lowering of self-esteem and lack of personal growth. When confronted by a principal about his or her motivational style, the enforcer can be argumentative and condescending.

The Abdicator

The abdicator style is characteristic of those teachers who are apathetic toward handling motivational problems and have little interest in their students. These teachers often feel burned out with the teaching profession
and are awaiting retirement or another position. Abdicators tolerate a great
deal of poor motivation in the classroom. Ultimately, they have low supporting and enforcing attributes.

Typical statements by the abdicator include "If they want to sleep, I just
let them sleep," "If they don't complete the work, I just flunk them; the heck
with them," and "You can lead a horse to water, but you can't make it drink;
if they come to class, fine; if they don't, it's their own problem." These
teachers tend to avoid confrontation in addressing motivational problems.

Abdicators are often characteristic of the stereotypical teacher who has
taught for many years and has become disgruntled with the profession.
The abdicator tends to be somewhat reclusive, does little to motivate students, and does not care whether the students behave or not. Their classes
tend to be disruptive.

When students recognize this motivational style in a teacher, they attempt to get away with as much as they can. Students will push the teacher
to the limit. They soon realize that the teacher has poor classroom management; consequently, they display little respect toward the teacher and
often become demotivated. This style of motivation can lead to student
demotivation, poor academic achievement, and class disruption. Not only
do these teachers have a low regard for maintaining high motivation, but
this apathy will carry over toward their attitude for student learning as
well. The teachers tend to have low support to the students and will avoid
negotiating with students, unless they have to.

Like the enforcer, the abdicator can create havoc for the school administrators. It is difficult for the principal to effectively deal with the abdicator, especially if this teacher is protected by tenure. Although the abdicator may do the minimum effort required as a teacher, his or her style of
motivating may not be serious enough to warrant discharge.

The Compromiser

The compromiser teacher is one who tends to engage in a great deal of
give-and-take in bargaining with his or her students. The compromiser

teacher appears to be more willing to compromise his or her own positions than those of the students. Therefore, these teachers can be somewhat wishy-washy and inconsistent. Examples of typical statements by the compromiser include "Dealing with students is a give-and-take process; otherwise, they'll shut down on you and you'll get nowhere with them" and "I guess I find myself working with the student and compromising all the time." Compromisers display moderate assertiveness and empathy toward students. They tend to be inconsistent in enforcing policies, and they come across to students as manipulative and confusing. At times, they may have concern in empathizing with students, whereas at other times they may embrace an assertive style.

There can be many negative consequences of this style. Students often become confused and do not know where they stand in dealing with the compromiser. Given the teacher's inconsistency in managing behavior, these teachers are often viewed by students as being wheeler-dealers. Students often become frustrated in seeking a balance between their own behavior and the expectations of the teacher. As a result, this style often creates conflict among the students. Students may feel pitted against other students and develop resentment among their classmates because of this inconsistency in enforcement of rules and policies.

The Supporter

The supporter-style teacher makes great efforts to talk with students about motivational problems and will leave a great deal of latitude. This teacher displays a high degree of empathy and concern for the student but shows little assertiveness. Also, this teacher is concerned about the personal feelings of the student.

Typical statements of the supporter include "I listen to my students, and if there are extenuating circumstances, I'll give them a break" and "I have a deep concern for the feelings of my kids and do my best to work with them; every kid is different and you can't treat students all the same." The supporter often takes a soothing and unassertive approach in handling motivational problems. Supporters tend to give students the benefit of the doubt and are often evasive and uncommitted to motivating them.

The negative consequences of this style are that students will often run over the teacher and that they may get away with low motivation. The classroom will typically be disruptive because the teacher places the needs of students over the need for rules and regulations. These teachers are concerned with ensuring that the students are comfortable and that there is an atmosphere of great care for students, versus the need for ensuring high performance and academic achievement. This type of teacher sacrifices student learning for personal attention and feelings of the student.

The Negotiator

The negotiator is a teacher who places a high value on a win-win approach to motivating students. These teachers have a high degree of both enforcing and supporting. They strive to develop a learning environment where students excel to their fullest potential, by balancing empathy and assertiveness with their students. These teachers make use of many approaches to motivate, such as parent–teacher conferences, listening to students, intrinsic and extrinsic motivators, and counseling sessions with their students.

The negotiator places high value on giving extra time after school to talk with students and parents in an effort to maintain a collaborative win-win environment. These teachers make statements such as "Working with the student involves a collective process of parents, teachers, and the student in coming to a consensus as to what is best for the student" and "I try to take an objective approach in counseling my students to find suitable motivators."

The negotiator is objective, committed, responsible, and takes initiative in motivating students. He or she does not subscribe to a zero-tolerance policy but recognizes that situations warrant different actions because of extenuating circumstances. A negotiator investigates the facts of a given motivational situation. Although negotiators value assertiveness in maintaining control, they do this with love and respect toward their students.

There are few negative consequences of the negotiator. These teachers have a high degree of commitment to maintaining motivation without belittling and intimidating students. They also attempt to be consistent as much as possible while recognizing individual needs. The negotiator style is not one of a compromiser but one of a collaborator.

Students respect this type of teacher because they know that the teacher has a great deal of empathy for all students. These teachers tend to develop an attitude of common stake in the classroom through trust, respect, and mutual concern among all. They expect students to treat them with respect, and they respect their students as well. Although the negotiator places a high value on rules and regulations, he or she also places a high value on student growth, flexibility, and appropriate freedom in the classroom. Also, the negotiator uses the best disciplinary approach given his or her students, his or her own style, and the situation.

7

Special Motivational Situations

DEALING WITH CONFLICT SITUATIONS

One of the important aspects in motivating students is the leader's ability to manage conflict. Conflict is common among students in schools. Snowden and Gorton (2002) describe conflict management as "efforts designed to prevent, ameliorate or resolve disagreements between and among individuals and groups" (p. 89). The leader's ability to effectively manage conflict has a direct relationship with the motivation of students. There are several sources of conflict in schools. Conflict can result from ineffective communications, roles, territorial issues, goals, stress, procedures and policies, and leadership.

Figure 7.1 shows an example of a survey that can be beneficial for educators to use in helping to identify sources of conflict within their schools. This instrument can be used in in-service workshops in which teachers first identify their individual rankings of the top 10 sources of conflict, followed by small-group consensus in ranking the top 10 conflict sources. Participants can also list other sources or causes of conflict. Discussion should then follow whereby the participants discuss each of the conflict sources and then develop action plans to help reduce conflict within their school.

Negative perceptions or prejudice given to students by educators can be demotivating for students. This perceived or real prejudice is a form of subtle punishment in the eyes of students and can lead to disciplinary misbehavior and apathy. Educators are often unaware of the perceived favoritism

Directions: Rank the sources of conflict from 1 to 10 (1 being the largest contributor and 10 being the least contributor). The first column is for individual students, the second for small groups.

Perceived teacher favoritism to students	_____	_____
Teacher demands upon student	_____	_____
Personality differences among students	_____	_____
Stress in student's life	_____	_____
Outside home and social issues	_____	_____
Students competition for attention or power	_____	_____
Rivalry gangs or student cliques	_____	_____
Change and new expectations	_____	_____
School or class environment (noise, condition)	_____	_____
Miscommunication among people	_____	_____
Please list any other sources or causes of conflict	_____	_____

Figure 7.1.   Sample Conflict Survey: Sources of Conflict

or prejudice that they may be giving to students. For example, the perception of favoritism can be as subtle as the lack of eye contact or the harshness of the educator's voice to students. For example, an educator may be more enthusiastic and positive to some students than to other students, which can be perceived as favoritism in their eyes. Therefore, teachers need to be aware of their communication and nonverbal behavior toward all students and try to be consistent to all students. Educator demands on students can also lead to demotivation, especially if students believe that an educator is placing excessive demands on them.

The personality differences among students can also be a source of conflict. Students' personalities (e.g., intuitor, thinker, feeler, and doer) can be different and can lead to different preferences in approaching team exercises that can lead to arguments. For example, if students are working on a team project and one student has the personality of a doer, he or she may be viewed as being too aggressive in wanting to accomplish the project by a student with the thinker personality style. The thinker student may think that the doer student is being too pushy and small-minded concerning the project. Likewise, the student's personality style of the feeler when working with the doer can cause conflict. The feeler may perceive the doer student as being insensitive toward him or her. Besides working in team projects, the normal interactions that students have socially with one another in school and out of school can also affect their motivation. For example, if students with different personality styles develop conflict outside the school, this conflict can also continue within the classroom, which can demotivate students.

Without a doubt, stress is common among students in today's schools. There are high demands placed on students by parents, society, community, administrators, and peers. For example, students are going through a physical and psychological growth and development process whereby their peer groups are important to them. Therefore, personal relationships can be a powerful factor in contributing to their self-esteem and self-concept. Their self-esteem can be positive or negative depending on their relationships with their peers. If a student has a boyfriend or girlfriend, this can positively or negatively affect his or her motivation in school. The relationship may distract him or her from focusing on schoolwork, and he or she may be less motivated to do work and more motivated to be with the boyfriend or girlfriend. The relationship can have a negative impact on motivating a student to perform well. On the other hand, it is possible that a positive relationship with a boyfriend or girlfriend can support a positive motivation. If the boyfriend or girlfriend foresees school to be important, the student may be motivated to perform well to maintain the respect and love.

The factors within a student's home and social pressures can have a direct impact in creating conflict within the student's classroom. If a student is experiencing difficulty within his or her home environment, such as an abusive parent, hostility within the family, or other relationship issues, the student may feel stressed and preoccupied with these issues and be demotivated in school. While in school, the student may have a difficult time focusing and caring about schoolwork when outside issues may be deemed more important. However, it is possible that the student may be motivated to perform well to avoid some of the negative aspects in life or to avoid thinking and feeling about these negative home problems.

The competition among students for attention or power can contribute positively or negatively toward the students' motivation. For example, if a student is competing among other students for good grades, he or she may be motivated to perform well in school. However, it is possible that if the student's peer group is more concerned with sports or social activities than school, then the student may be negatively influenced and have less motivation. Some students may seek power through their high academic achievement. For example, if a student is concerned about being ranked in the top 10% of his or her school, then he or she may be motivated to achieve a higher class ranking to obtain more power. However, if a student's ranking is low and somewhat embarrassing to the student, he or she may actually be demotivated and not care about school and thus divert his or her interests elsewhere.

In some schools the presence of gangs and student cliques can present a major problem for motivating a student for good learning. If a student is more concerned about protecting himself or herself because of the fear of gangs, or if a student is involved in gangs, he or she may be less motivated to perform well in school. The involvement in gangs can be a negative influence on a student's motivation for schoolwork because gangs generally do not place a high value on academic achievement. Student cliques, to a lesser degree than rival gangs, can also present a problem. If a student is involved with a clique that is unconcerned about learning, then this can have a negative motivation for the student. However, if the clique is involved with extracurricular activities and academic clubs, then the student may be motivated to achieve and learn as much as possible.

Managing change and adapting to change is a critical factor in a student's motivation. Stability can be the enemy of survival. Change is inevitable, and those who fail to effectively manage change can have negative consequences on their motivation for learning. For example, there are several situations in which a student may be affected by change, such as a family's moving to another school district or changes within a school district causing a student to be transferred to a new school. The student's ability to develop new relationships and adapt to this change is directly related to his or her motivation. In these situations students develop new expectations for performance as well as establish familiarity with the school and personal relationships. Besides changing from one school to another, just changes within a student's life can have significant impact on his or her motivation. As a student develops, he or she goes through changes and is able to successfully adapt to these changes to different degrees. If a student experiences weight problems because of physiological change, this can affect a student's motivation toward learning.

The school or class environment also contributes to a student's motivation. If a student is in a classroom with a great deal of noise and stimuli, the student who does not adapt well to this environment may be less motivated to learn. The environment may be distracting to the student, and his or her ability to focus on learning can be hampered. For example, a student who is in a public classroom that is highly enriching with experiences and stimuli may find it difficult if he or she is used to a private school where a traditional instructional approach with less stimuli is used.

A student also may be affected if the temperature of the environment is compromised. For example, if the temperature is either too hot or too cold, the student may have a difficult time focusing on learning.

One of the contributors to conflict is that of miscommunication among students and educators. Human beings are social creatures who communicate on a daily basis. Each of their interactions often involves a negotiating element that can cause miscommunication to take place. For example, if a teacher makes a statement to a student and it is misunderstood, the student may have ill feelings toward the teacher and become demotivated. Likewise, miscommunication can take place among students.

There are many forms of communication, such as written, spoken, nonverbal, that can affect a student's understanding of rules, regulations, and policies. For example, if information is communicated to a student about a homework assignment, the misinterpretation of the information may have a negative effect on the student's performance and demotivate him or her. Likewise, perhaps one of the most significant causes of miscommunication is that of the grapevine communication network. This is an informal communication system in schools in which rumors start and can contribute to misunderstandings and miscommunication.

There are many causes of conflict, such as role incongruence, goal differences, territorial issues, and desire for power and control. For example, conflict can result because of role incongruence (e.g., educator demonstrates that behavior is inappropriate). The educator needs to understand that the role that he or she serves is that of a professional in the eyes of people and thus cannot conduct himself or herself to the contrary. The educator should behave according to his or her job description and the expected role of the educator so that there is not a creation of role ambiguity that confuses a student, which can contribute to demotivating him or her. Therefore, the job of an educator to be an effective leader and motivator to students is a challenging one. The direct relationship of successfully managing conflict to motivate students is a critical aspect of education.

The inability to effectively manage conflict can result in many negative consequences. Some examples of results of ineffective conflict management follow:

- Poor student morale
- Open hostility
- Discipline problems

- Poor student attitudes
- Lack of student motivation
- Disruption in learning
- Wasted time
- Stress and frustration
- Lack of teamwork
- Lack of respect for each other

For example, if students are experiencing conflict with one another in the classroom, open hostility can result. These behaviors do not only cause disruption in the entire classroom learning process but also lead to verbal and physical confrontations among the students. This negative environment can lead to demotivation for the students involved, as well as all students.

THE TEACHER–STUDENT CONFLICT NEEDS MODEL

There are several different techniques for resolving conflict that can be utilized by the leader. For example, Figure 7.2 illustrates a teacher–

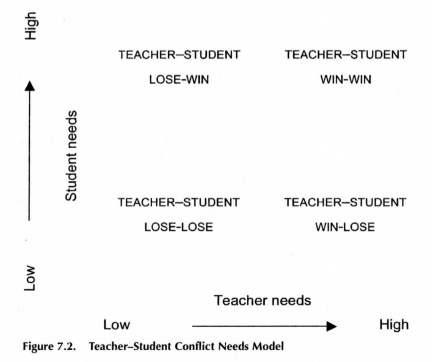

Figure 7.2.   Teacher–Student Conflict Needs Model

student conflict needs model that can be effective in understanding the underlying needs of conflict and achieving to resolution. This model suggests that the teacher and student both have needs that they would like to meet. If a teacher forces his or her needs to be met (e.g. high need level) at the expense of the student's needs (e.g. low need level), then a win-lose situation may arise (as illustrated in the first quadrant of the model).

The Win-Win Quadrant

The win-win quadrant illustrates a position where both the teacher and the student have a high desire to accommodate their needs. In this situation a collaborative effort can begin with the student and teacher in an effort to resolve the conflict matter. This can result in a win-win situation for both the teacher and the student and may be the best approach to use in attempting to resolve conflict. The essence of this situation is that through consensus the two parties can negotiate and come to a resolution that is the best for maintaining student motivation and respect for the needs of the teacher in the learning process.

The Lose-Win Quadrant

The lose-win quadrant of the model illustrates a situation where the student has a high desire for needs being met whereas the teacher's needs are low. In this situation this becomes a lose-win position for the student. For example, if the student is expressing a strong need to obtain additional time to complete homework and the teacher does not want to take the time to argue or negotiate with the student and just accommodates the student's request, then the need level of the student is met. This situation may be good in helping to motivate the student for good performance. However, in certain situations this may be negative in that it reinforces the student's behavior that is undesirable.

The Lose-Lose Quadrant

However, if both the teacher and the student have low needs in resolving conflict, then the likely outcome may be a lose-lose situation (as illustrated in the fourth quadrant of the model). This might be a situation where both the student and the teacher have disrespect toward each other and would rather avoid each other. However, it might be used in a situation where there is trivial conflict and each person wants to avoid the conflict so that it does not escalate. In the latter situation, it is possible that the conflict may in time be resolved and a normal relationship can be achieved.

COMMUNICATION STRATEGIES FOR RESOLVING CONFLICT

There are several communication strategies that a teacher can use to help resolve conflict. Some of these include the following:

- Anticipation
- Paraphrasing
- Appeal to interests
- Silence
- Limit-setting parameters

Anticipation

The use of the anticipation approach is especially good when dealing with one-on-one conflict. In this situation, if an educator anticipates that a student will have a negative response to a conflict issue, the educator might begin by stating, "I know we have had difficulty discussing this issue in the past; however, you are very important to me, and I did not mean any disrespect to you, so I was wondering if it would be okay if we could further discuss the situation." By using the anticipation strategy, the teacher, in essence, anticipates the student's reaction and tries to reduce the negative feelings that the student might have. This can be an effective technique in building positive relationships.

Paraphrasing

The use of paraphrasing is a common communication technique in which the educator simply puts in his or her own words what the student is stating. For example, if the student states that he or she is having difficulty with the content and is uncomfortable asking questions in front of his or her classmates, the educator might state, "If you feel reluctant to talk in front of your peers because you may feel they will think poorly of you, I will be happy to work with you after class." In using this technique, the educator effectively paraphrases the student's statements and reestablishes communication with the student.

Appeal to Interests

Another technique, appeal to interests, is a common one that can be used for one-on-one conflict resolution. An educator might begin a conversation by identifying the student's interest and using it to start the conversation. For example, if the educator knows the student is good in sports, the teacher might state, "I know you are an outstanding athlete and a hard worker, so I thought that you would have the same passion for our class subject." Introducing the student's interest in sports and hard work can help to bridge communication in resolving a motivational issue within the classroom.

Silence

The fourth technique is the use of silence. Never underestimate the power of allowing a student to begin talking about a conflict issue. Also, if an educator is slow to speak (through use of silence), the student may be more inclined to talk and resolve conflict.

Limit-Setting Parameters

An example of limit-setting parameters is when an educator states, "I can do this, but I can't do that." This allows the educator to negotiate with the student in resolving conflict, but it places a limit on which resolution or agreement can occur. If the student wants to achieve more time to complete an assignment, the educator may say, "I can give you one more day, but I can't give you more than that." Limit-setting parameters are a good technique in introducing one's position and beginning the start of negotiations in resolving conflict.

THINGS TO KEEP IN MIND

In attempting to resolve conflict, a teacher should always keep in mind the concept of the iceberg phenomenon. Much like a real iceberg, where only the tip of the frozen material can be seen and a majority of the ice is underneath, so is it true for conflict between people. Often, the presence of conflict is indicative of underlying issues. On the surface a student may avoid a teacher; however, the real issues of conflict may be deep within. Therefore, a teacher should not just assume that the apparent issue is the only source of the conflict; he or she should explore other issues that may be contributing to the conflict.

There are many principles in resolving conflict with a student, such as careful listening and empathizing with the student, searching for hidden meanings, separating the important issues from the unimportant ones, and approaching the conflict from a collaborative standpoint. Educators should also avoid common phrases that evoke conflict and can unmotivate students, such as the following:

- What is wrong with you this time?
- What you need to do is this . . . !
- You always lie to me; here we go again!
- If you really cared about yourself, you would . . .
- You just want attention again, so you should . . .
- I don't care what you think; you need to . . .
- Don't you care about anything but . . .
- Here we go again; what are you thinking?
- I am at my limit with you; you are impossible.
- So, you think you can change your attitude?

An effective educator is able to control his or her emotional intelligence. Essentially, this means understanding what triggers a negative emotion that causes the educator to respond inappropriately to a student. These negative statements can be damaging to the student and can unmotivate him or her. For example, "always" and "never" are words that generally need to be avoided because they can provoke argumentative communications.

When communicating with a student, it is important to use active listening techniques and words that demonstrate good listening. Statements that are encouraging, clarifying, empathizing, supportive, and sensitive often form a good foundation for communication and resolving conflicts.

It is often helpful to use a problem-solving approach to resolving conflict when talking with a student. Resolving conflict between an educator and a student includes the following seven steps:

1. Describe the situation—suspend judgment.
2. Humanize the situation—respect the other person.
3. Clarify the conflict issue—be clear on the conflict.
4. Recognize emotions—avoid put-downs.
5. Recognize positions—empathize with the person.
6. Negotiate resolution—consider win-win approach.
7. Extend appreciation—end on a positive note.

The first step in resolving conflict is to describe the situation. It is important to suspend judgment and accept students as they are and not to antagonize them. Anticipate the emotional reaction from the student and be ready to de-escalate any conflict. In the second step, it is important to make sure to humanize the situation. You should approach the situation from a win-win standpoint and acknowledge the student, giving respect and courtesy. The third step involves clearly presenting the conflict issue to be addressed. Identify the issue and avoid putting down the student. Be careful to note any underlying issues and reactions by the student. The fourth step involves recognizing emotions. In this step, remember not to state any put-downs to the other person and to be sensitive to your own emotions that may be provoked and the emotions of the student. This step especially requires having good emotional intelligence.

The fifth step, recognizing positions, is where you need to empathize with the student. You might state, "I can understand how you would feel" and other statements that support a collaborative resolution to the matter. Avoid emotionalism and defensiveness. Always try to be open and personal, particularly at this step.

The sixth step involves negotiating resolution. This is essentially the step where the content of the issue is discussed and negotiated. Hopefully, a collaborative resolution can result. The last step includes extending appreciation. The conflict resolution should end on a positive note. Agreement and expectations should be clear, and, if necessary, follow-up measures should be established.

The need to understand how to manage conflict is essential in helping students maintain and achieve positive motivation in the classroom. Learning basic strategies for managing conflict can be one of the more useful strategies in helping students to perform to their highest ability and achieve success.

MANAGING STRESSFUL SITUATIONS

One of the more significant factors that affect an educator's ability to motive students is stress. Stress plays a role in everyone's life, and an educator's ability to manage stress is directly related to his or her leadership effectiveness. Algozzine and Jazzar (2006) state, "Stress will be a condition of twenty-first century education leadership as full scale reform increases and more demands and new policy initiatives are produced" (p. 22).

Stress is generally considered to be bad. However, stress can be good as well. The notion that stress is good or bad can often be determined by how an educator deals with it in his or her mind. Whether stress is good or bad, its physiological symptoms can be the same—increased breathing, lower body temperature, increased heart rate, and so on. Therefore, an example of good stress might be anticipating marriage, attending a sports event, or receiving an award. Examples of bad stress may include participating in a disciplinary conference, losing a job, or going through a divorce. In both cases similar physiological symptoms occur. Therefore, the educator's ability to think of stress as a positive factor and deal with it positively in one's mind is one of the keys to effectively managing stress.

Good stress can stimulate performance and increase a leader's ability to excel. However, the serious repercussions of bad stress, when not managed well, are evident throughout society, such as health problems, strained relationships, and hostility.

An educator needs to understand that stress is a natural reaction—the so-called fight or flight syndrome. When faced with stress, human beings have the ability to either flee or fight it out. However, in modern society, too often a person needs to just sit there and take it. Therefore, effectively using stress management techniques is even more important.

Another principle of stress is that it is individual. What may cause stress in one person does not cause stress in another. For example, between two people, the ideal vacation can consist of opposite locations. One may prefer a hot sunny beach whereas another may desire an active mountain-climbing experience. Dwelling on stress generally increases stress.

When experiencing stress, the negative talking about stress can cause more harm. Stress can be self-induced. Many people needlessly self-impose stress. For example, if an educator is getting distressed in anticipation of a difficult discussion with a student, this behavior may be futile.

There are many causes of stress that affect educators (see Table 7.1). Causes of stress for school educators can be categorized under four headings: school stressors, personal stressors, student stressors, and work stressors. Some of the typical demands regarding school stressors range from constant changes and administrative demands to excessive paperwork and need to reach performance standards. For example, as increased state and federal standards are imposed on teachers, the need to produce higher academic results increases. This, in turn, causes added pressure and stress. Personal stressors range from health problems to an unfulfilling job. A typical example is a teacher who has been teaching for several years and is experiencing burnout. Unless it is managed well, this personal stressor can affect the educator's effectiveness.

Table 7.1.   **Types of Stress That Affect Educators**

School Stressors	Personal Stressors
School change	Health problems
Administrative demands	Facing retirement
Financial constraints	Unfulfilled job
Performance standards	Loss of a loved one
Excessive paperwork	Financial problems
Student Stressors	*Work Stressors*
Student demands	Problems with parents
Student misbehavior	Safety and security
Student apathy	Personality differences
Student violence	Work conflicts
Student poor performance	Legal problems

Student stressors include the obvious demands placed on teachers by students because of misbehavior, apathy, or poor performance. This situation can be defined as goal incongruence in that the educator desires to have high performance or to meet a specific behavioral standard and the students have alternative ones. Work stressors include typical stressors caused by personality differences among staff members, parent dealings, and safety and security concerns within the school building.

Like leaders, students face a variety of stressors as well. Student stressors comprise four categories: social, personal, school, and performance (see Table 7.2).

Typical social stressors that affect students include peer competition, parental and societal demands, and general society change. For example, a student who is going through a socialization stage in life will be greatly affected by the need to maintain peer standards of dress and conduct. Students also may be pressured into participating in extracurricular activities and outside interests that cause significant time demands. Personal stressors, especially important for students during this development age, include self-esteem issues, appearance, and dealing with sexuality. Especially for young teenagers, the concern regarding their appearance and how they are accepted by their peers, is of larger personal significance.

School-related stressors include teacher and administrator demands, the need to adhere to rules and policies of the school, and dealing with the conditions of the school. If the school is overly crowded, then just getting

Table 7.2.   Stressors That Affect Students

Social Stressors	*Personal Stressors*
Peer competition	Personal development
Society demands	Self-esteem issues
Parental pressures	Appearance and health
Relationship demands	Dealing with sexuality
Change and conflicts	Personal value conflicts
Student Stressors	*Performance Stressors*
Teacher demands	Parents demands
Teacher expectations	State demands
Rules and procedures	Career interests
School policies	Scheduling conflicts
School conditions	Time demands

from class to class can cause stress for students. The last category, performance stressors, includes the demands placed on students by parents and the state boards of education. In addition, students are beginning to explore their career interests in life, which can often be a difficult challenge during this time.

It is important to recognize that stress can involve physical, mental, and emotional sources. The ability to recognize the source of stress (e.g., physical, mental, or emotional) is important because once the source is determined, then the student's doing more of the other source can sometimes reduce the stress. For example, if a person is emotionally stressed, then performing a vigorous physical workout can help reduce the emotional stress. Likewise, if an educator is mentally stressed, he or she can watch an emotional movie and this can help him or her to relax. One example of this concept is how prisoners of war performed mental exercises to help reduce their high degrees of emotional stress during their capture. Likewise, if a person is physically stressed, then reading a book may help reduce the physical stress.

Symptoms of stress can be categorized under feelings, physiological, and behavioral (see Table 7.3). Typical feelings associated with stress range from feelings of insecurity and depression to impatience and irritability. A leader who is experiencing stress needs to understand that the typical feelings of depression may be the result of stress found on his or her job, and the need to deal with the stress can in turn reduce these negative feelings. Typical physiological symptoms include body aches and pains and stomach dysfunction. It is typical for a person who is experiencing stress to develop stomach problems such as diarrhea or constipation. With this in mind, understanding strategies of stress management can help to reduce these physiological problems. The result of stress can be behavioral

Table 7.3. **Categories of Stressors**

Feelings	Physiological	Behavioral
Insecurity	Neck tension	Smoking
Depression	Back tension	Alcohol abuse
Frustration	Stomachaches	Poor listening
Impatience	Diarrhea	Nervousness
Irritability	Constipation	Forgetfulness
Inadequacy	Headaches	Poor sleeping

symptoms. Often, people exhibit inappropriate behaviors while being under stress, such as alcohol abuse, poor listening, and forgetfulness. When a person is under stress, he or she typically does not listen well to people. Therefore, understanding the feelings, physiological, and behavioral symptoms of stress can be a first step in learning to manage stress effectively.

Although there are many causes of stress for educators, fortunately, there are many strategies that can be employed to reduce stressors in life. The ability to identify causes of stress and then incorporate stress strategies is the foundation of managing stress. Some strategies are more effective than others for a particular kind of stress, and an educator needs to select the one that gives him or her the best results.

There are many quick tension relievers than can be used to reduce tension, such as massaging the top of your forehead or back of the neck. Taking time to stretch your muscles and complete a series of deep breathing exercises can be helpful throughout the day. These techniques can be particularly useful for students when they are forced to sit in chairs most of the day. The need to stretch and obtain some physical exercise can be beneficial, and given that educators and students may not always be able to partake in aggressive physical activity, these tension relaxers can provide some help.

Having a good friend or colleague at work can be helpful in talking about school problems and reducing your stress. This can also be therapeutic during times of emotional distress. Talking with colleagues in the teachers lounge or in between classes can help people express mutual concerns and give one another support by listening, caring, empathizing, venting feelings, and giving emotional support. After-school social events can also be effective in building supportive relationships and helping to discuss mutual concerns.

Human beings have the tendency to silently talk to themselves, especially during stressful situations. Self-talk can be positive or negative. Negative self-talk can be destructive when people dwell on their stress situation, and it can produce unreasonable expectations. It is not healthy to focus on the stressful situation and create mountains out of molehills. However, the ability to think positively and talk to oneself in a positive manner can be helpful in reducing stress. People, however, have more difficulty in practicing positive self-talk than negative self-talk. Therefore, one of the best strategies to prevent negative self-talk is to picture a bright red stop sign and say to yourself "Stop" and then think positive thoughts.

There is an old expression: "We are what we eat." Similarly, the expression "We feel what we think" can apply. Whether an event is real or not, the physiological reactions are often the same. For example, if a person is having a bad dream and awakens in a cold sweat, the body is reacting to the negative thoughts as if they were actually occurring. The dream is not reality, but the body sometimes does not differentiate between them. Therefore, it is important to reduce negative thoughts and to concentrate on positive mental images. For example, during stressful situations, a person might think of a pleasant environment, such as a tropical beach or paradise or another favorite vacation spot. This visualization can help one to think positive thoughts and thus reduce physiologic stress.

People tend to have one of two types of personality: Personality A or Personality B. Personality A individuals are those who have an intense drive and aggressiveness and are impatient and competitive. Personality B people are more patient, less time-conscious, and more relaxed and complacent. Understanding your personality style and tolerance to stress is important to reducing it. Personality A people may be more prone to stress, especially when they are not accomplishing performance at desired expectations. It is possible that Personality A individuals may experience more health problems given their impulsiveness and desire for high expectations. Therefore, a strategy that can be used if you are a Personality A individual is to develop less-intense drive and competitiveness while completing work. This, in effect, can help to reduce some of the high expectations and in turn reduce your stress.

One of the more common and effective techniques for managing stress is meditation and relaxation. Your ability to find a quiet spot to reduce all outside thoughts from your mind and simply relax by concentrating on one individual word or point can help to reduce stress. There are numerous meditation techniques, and learning these techniques and developing expertise can be beneficial.

A strategy that can be performed at the end of a school day is called reflection. This technique is performed by finding a quiet spot and simply reflecting on the day's activities and determining how well you managed your work day. Hendricks (2006) states, "The definition of reflection goes beyond the notion that reflection is merely thinking about a problem. Instead, thinking about a problem is a first step of reflection" (p. 23). Reflection requires a realistic appraisal of your effectiveness in managing your work, whether good or bad. For example, if you experienced a disciplinary problem with a student, thinking about how well you managed this situation and finding better ways to manage similar disciplinary problems in the future can help to reduce stress. Reflection is a good process of examining how well you have coped with stress and the work tasks of the day and of finding better ways to perform.

The flow of electricity is common to life. Both have positive and negative elements that are essential for producing energy. Electricity must have positives and negatives, and life can also be viewed as enriching when one realizes that there will be both ups and downs. Therefore, your ability to understand that life will have problems and to learn to grow from these problems can help to reduce future stress.

People have a tendency to distort things during crises, producing an all-or-nothing attitude. This can develop into a self-defeatist attitude and produce even more stress. Avoiding jumping to conclusions or overemotionalizing every situation can help one to discern significant issues from unimportant ones. Remember, we are not always saving the world, and getting worked up over little things is senseless. With this in mind, it is sometimes helpful to think of people who are worse off than yourself. This, in turn, can allow you to be more thankful for your own situation, and your problems will seem to be much less significant.

If an educator is experiencing job stress and feeling burned out, one way that he or she can manage the situation is to think of the job within the context of life. All jobs have good and bad aspects to them. Recognizing the many good aspects can help in understanding the context that the role of a teacher requires. An educator cannot select only the good parts of the job. Therefore, recognizing that there are good and bad aspects can help in accepting the job and the role as a teacher. For example, if a teacher dislikes disciplining students, he or she must understand that the role of an educator is that of a leader and disciplinarian, and understanding this within the context of teaching can help to reduce stress.

One of the strongest drives of human beings is that of fear. Fear can inspire or hinder performance. For example, if a teacher is nervous about meeting with a group of irate parents, then the mere resisting of the event is sometimes worse than the event itself. So, instead of resisting the encounter with the parents, which may cause increased shaking and perspiration, and fighting the fear, one can do the opposite and simply accept it. This, in turn, can help reduce the shaking and perspiration. In other words, it is the resistance of the event itself that is causing the shaking and perspiration, rather than the actual event. This technique can be useful in situations dealing with people and confrontations. It can also help to allow you to be calmer during these stressful encounters.

When under stress, people often resort to poor behaviors that negatively affect health. Substance abuse, excessive eating, lack of sleep, and lack of exercise are just some of the poor behaviors. Not only do these poor behaviors reduce one's effectiveness in managing stress, but they can cause illness and sickness, which compound the stress situation. Therefore, recognizing one's behaviors and health habits is the first step in selecting more appropriate behaviors to reduce stress. For example, instead of going home after work and watching television and drinking alcohol to relax, it is better to participate in an exercise program and eat a well-balanced meal. A simple thing such as obtaining sufficient sleep can help to rejuvenate a person and reduce stress. Without sufficient sleep, the body cannot manage stress well and recover.

Although these strategies can be effective in helping an educator reduce stress, they can also be helpful in teaching students to reduce stress as well. An effective leader can recognize when a student is experiencing stress and thus help coach him or her in reducing stress. If an educator is witnessing a student being frustrated and stressed in the classroom, he or she might simply ask the student to stay after class for a few minutes to discuss his or her situation and offer a few suggestions. If time is unavailable, an educator may ask permission to call the student during the evening and talk to him or her to offer some suggestions. This can help not only reduce the student's stress but promote positive relationships and academic performance.

DEALING WITH LEGAL SITUATIONS

An educator's practice in motivating and disciplining students must take into account legal considerations. The ever-increasing complexity of state and federal laws and regulations regarding student management can be overwhelming for any educator. Algozzine and Jazzar (2006) state, "With these litigious conditions impacting education today, numerous questions for educational administrators, both current and future, surface" (p. 117). Therefore, an educator's attempt to motivate students and maintain discipline must be operated within existing laws and student rights. As these laws change over time, educators need to stay current with these changes. Any educator who has experienced a lawsuit well understands the emotional anxiety associated with defending it. Defending a lawsuit can take a significant amount of school resources, such as time, money, and people. The best policy to practice is a defensive one that takes in account understanding of student rights, school policies, state and federal laws, and prevention of litigation and lawsuits.

Defensive teaching practices entails understanding and enforcing the legal requirements of all educators in motivating students, the legal rights of students, and the rights of educators in the school. Some of the legal requirements expected of teachers include the prevention of teacher insubordination, incompetence, and criminal acts. A teacher may be found insubordinate when he or she fails to follow school policies regarding motivation, teaching practices, or the direct orders of administrators, unless the life or safety of a person is at risk. For example, if a teacher is trying to motivate a student to perform to a higher standard and is using coercive strategies, this practice may violate school policies and state and federal laws regarding harassment and inflicting undue emotional stress on students.

Administrators must also conduct regular performance evaluations of teachers and be responsible for teachers' performance, which may include evaluating a teacher's ability in motivating students. If a teacher is found to be incompetent because of his or her failure to properly discipline students or motivate them to learn, and the administrator tolerates this incompetence, then the principal may also be held liable. The school must also protect against teachers who are involved in criminal acts—especially, acts involving sexual immorality, violence, and drugs—to protect the welfare of students. Students have the right to be protected from teachers who are involved in such criminal acts.

The Bill of Rights allows protection for students to exercise basic freedoms under the U.S. Constitution. The amendments to the Constitution of the United States also provide guidelines regarding student rights. These laws safeguard students' freedom to expression as long as there is not disruption to the school. The educator may be cautious in forbidding student free speech, especially if it is on a controversial topic, unless it can be shown that there is substantial disruption to the school. For example, students' participation in handing out flyers expressing opinions regarding social events or their organizing peaceful rallies or demonstrations may be allowed under the U.S. Constitution. Many organizations have objectives to ensure individual rights, such as the American Civil Liberties Union or National Lawyers Guild.

When motivating students, educators need to be careful that they do not discriminate on the basis of race or gender (Title IV of the Civil Rights Act). If a teacher is encouraging a student to perform better in school and uses phrases such as "Come on, your poor performance is a discredit to your race" or "Just because you are a girl doesn't mean you can't perform better," these statements may be of a discriminatory nature and a violation of student rights under federal law.

Teachers also need to be concerned with the federal law concerning access to student records (Family Education Rights and Privacy Act). This law grants parents and students who are 18 years old or older the right to examine personal student records. Students who are under 18 are also granted permission to review their student records if a parent gives written permission or if the school policy allows this practice. Therefore, this law has ramifications in student motivation when educators attempt to review records and discuss personal information with students in an effort to ascertain behavior and academic performance to make improvements.

Schools may also be liable for compensatory damages if injury is incurred by students due to unreasonable or inappropriate motivational strategies or excessive discipline, physical punishment, threats or coercion, or punishment that causes harm to students. Therefore, the use of corporal punishment has generally been outlawed and is a violation of many state and school board policies.

Educators must be concerned with ensuring student safety and providing reasonable care and guidelines for students while on school property and while off the school premises if the activities are related to school events. For example, if a teacher wants to motivate his or her students and takes the students on a field trip, then a degree of liability is encountered by the teacher and school. The teacher must also be careful to select appropriate motivational strategies without causing harm to the student.

Due process is another right that many students are granted in the school system. Students must be guaranteed some type of due process for their actions that may result in disciplinary actions or expulsion. Schools must take into account appropriate action for a given offense, taking into consideration the characteristics of the student, such as possible disability, prior disciplinary history, and school policies. For example, the Education for All Handicapped Children Act (Public Law 94-142) is a law that has been expanded to a more current law known as the Individuals With Disabilities Education Act (1990), which ensures that disabled students receive appropriate public education without discrimination. Therefore, these laws attempt to remove discrimination against disabled students that may otherwise cause the students to become demotivated and, to say the least, fail to receive an adequate education. There are many categories of disability, ranging from autism, deafness, emotional disturbances, mental disabilities, speech, and visual impairments.

If a teacher is attempting to discipline a student for poor motivation, reasonable disciplinary action should be given that does not disrupt the student's academic process for a given disciplinary offense. Schools should refrain from administering group punishment for an individual student's disciplinary act or offense.

Schools should also utilize a progressive disciplinary approach, which affords students due process for actions committed, ranging from severe to most severe. Schools should also consider mitigating and extenuating circumstances when deciding on disciplinary action for student apathy and unsatisfactory work performance because of motivational issues. Students should be given due process and should not be summarily transferred to other schools. For example, some schools have supported basic safeguards for due process based on federal and state laws, such as allowing students to have a brief review process, having clear policies for discipline and for administering discipline, an opportunity for students to appeal a decision, and protection of confidential information.

A process to help ensure that a school has an effective behavioral policy is to clearly delineate the responsibilities of teachers and to give them necessary authority in carrying out their role. The responsibility of teachers in ensuring that students behave properly is grounded under the jurisdiction of the school policy. While under the jurisdiction of the school, teachers are similar to parents—that is, *in loco parentis* (in place of the parent). Therefore it is necessary for teachers to have the responsibility and authority to property ensure that students behave according to the standards of the school. Although teachers may have authority, they must not participate in arbitrary, capricious, or discriminatory acts against students. In making decisions regarding disciplinary matters, teachers must always consider the circumstances of the students, such as age, emotional stability, physical and mental disabilities, and grade level. Therefore, teachers must be well trained in handling disciplinary matters, especially as they relate to the motivational levels of students, and they must be granted wide discretion in administering disciplinary actions against these students based on mitigating circumstances.

Schools have a responsibility to provide education for married or pregnant students. These students must not be excluded from extracurricular activities or academic activities unless harm can come to the students given their conditions. Therefore, a teacher may not take disciplinary action against a student because he or she believes that a pregnant student has immoral character. Recent laws have also supported the notion that pregnant students may fall under the definition of a disabled person. Likewise, various state and federal laws protect the rights of married students that participate in extracurricular activities. Students should also not be coerced or threatened by teachers for desiring to become married or pregnant.

The Supreme Court has upheld the right of a school to develop appropriate procedures of student conduct and to have authority to discipline students for misbehavior involving vulgar or profane language. Schools should not tolerate obscene, rude, or profane language or gestures. For example, if a student is becoming frustrated with his or her inability to perform and expresses vulgar language, this behavior should not be tolerated. Any offensive language or gesture that does not demonstrate the proper respect toward school or people can be a basis for disciplinary action. Inappropriate language or gestures can also agitate and incite other students to misbehave.

Therefore, the need to understand basic school policies as well as state and federal laws is important for the teacher in motivating and disciplining students. Some of the common laws regarding student rights and responsibilities include the following:

Public Law 93-380 (1974)
Education for All Handicapped Children Act (1975, also known as Public Law 94-142)
Section 504 Rehabilitation Act (1973)

Americans With Disabilities Education Act (1990)
Individuals With Disabilities Education Act Amendments (1997)
Title IV of the Civil Rights Act (1964)
Pregnancy and Discrimination Act (1978)
Occupational Safety and Health Act (1970)
Equal Employment Opportunity Act (1972)

MOTIVATING STUDENTS WITH SPECIAL NEEDS

Individuals are unique people with different motivational needs. What may motivate one student may not motivate another. Motivation is based on the factors that contribute to an individual and what he or she believes are important to motivate him or her to learn. Schools consist of a multiplicity of students with diverse backgrounds, and the need to recognize students' individuality is the first step in motivating them. Brown and Green (2006) state, "Researchers have suggested that special attention be paid to the needs of culturally diverse learners and learners with disabilities. Designing with diverse learners in mind has become a popular topic" (p. 133). Although there are numerous types of students in schools today, most of them can be categorized into basic dimensions, such as students with disabilities, gifted students, students with language barriers, and students with low self-esteem. Jensen and Kiley (2005) state, "Of course, not everyone is motivated by the same things. Think how the teaching/learning process is structured. For one thing, students are more likely to buy in to the learning process when they feel they have some say in it" (p. 17).

There are many students with various disabilities in the nation. These students represent a major challenge for education to ensure that they receive the most effective instruction given the financial resources available. Motivating students with disabilities requires special attention and consideration for how these students learn. The federal law titled Individuals With Disabilities Education Act, which was passed in 1990, was a follow-up to Public Law 94-142, and it gives basic principles for structuring learning for disabled students. Boyle and Weishaar (2001) state that this act "is based on a foundation of six principles: Zero Reject/Child Find, nondiscriminatory testing, individual education plan, least restrictive environment, procedural due process, and parental participation" (p. 3). Therefore, structuring the lesson plan that best accommodates students with disabilities is the first step in helping to motivate them.

Depending on the type of disability and the individual needs of the student, different motivators should be selected. Several motivational strategies that can be used with students with disabilities include the following:

- Use a combination of extrinsic and intrinsic rewards.
- Structure the learning exercises to students' interests.
- Use multiple intelligences to tailor to special needs.
- Use methods of behavioral skills modeling.
- Incorporate collaborative learning exercises.
- Use engaging exercises to maintain attention.
- Give tangible rewards for positive efforts.
- Give significant praise for achievements.
- Use multimedia and technology to aide instruction.
- Reward students incrementally.
- Give a lot of encouragement.

One of the more popular theories in which to help motivate students is that of multiple intelligences (Gardner, 1983). Gardner articulated eight basic intelligences, consisting of special, kinesthetic, musical, linguistic, mathematical, interpersonal, intrapersonal, and naturalistic. For example, a student who has difficulty learning in several areas but is gifted in music may be motivated through using songs, learning different tunes, and developing music to learn the material. On the other hand, if a student has strong kinesthetic abilities, he or she may best be motivated to learn through use of dance, constructing projects, and other physical-skill-learning activities. The ability of a teacher to identify a student's natural ability and use this as a means to motivate the student can be helpful in developing his or her competencies. The teacher should also remember that his or her expectations toward disabled students can have a profound effect on the selection of learning strategies and the student's performance. A teacher may develop specific bias or have limited expectations toward disabled students that can negatively affect the disabled student's performance. Therefore, the teacher must recognize his or her own expectations and how they may affect students' learning and motivation.

Some other strategies for motivating these students include using engaging exercises that promote inquiry, problem-solving investigations, and media and technology based instruction that can motivate students and help compensate for learning deficiencies. Other techniques include giving sufficient encouragement, praising students for their achievements, using behavior-skill-modeling techniques, and incorporating a combination of extrinsic and intrinsic rewards.

MOTIVATING GIFTED STUDENTS

Motivating students who are educationally gifted is a significant challenge for teachers. Gifted students need to be challenged with higher-level thinking and learning strategies. The process of learning (how knowledge is obtained) is defined as *epistemology*. This philosophy of science describes how people acquire knowledge through basically two methods, called *quantitative* and *qualitative*. Quantitative learning is based on scientific inquiry and is objective, and it uses numerical data to describe phenomena and statistical analysis to make conclusions. Qualitative learning is naturalistic and emergent, and it typically consists of words to express learning, studies in natural settings, and theories and concepts. Some gifted students may be motivated to learn by using quantitative methods such as math and science, which are numerical. Students who are gifted in qualitative learning are motivated through natural inquiry. Therefore, a teacher should recognize the gifts of these students and structure learning activities that support their self-motivation. If a student is gifted in mathematics, he or she may be motivated through use of quantitative analysis. However, a student who is motivated through theoretical and conceptual studies may be suited for qualitative learning approaches. Their self-motivation will be correlated with their type of intellectual gift. Some of the motivational strategies for gifted students are as follows:

- Accelerate the learning pace giving intrinsic recognition.
- Encourage self-reflection on learning experiences.
- Use methods of inquiry and investigation.
- Foster mentoring of other students for personal satisfaction.
- Use multiple instructional methods.

- Emphasize love of learning versus tangible rewards.
- Continue positive reinforcement for achievements.
- Use engaging instruction and self-paced exercises.
- Incorporate independent troubleshooting.
- Encourage heuristic learning methods.

Given that gifted students require higher-level thinking strategies, teachers may introduce and promote different ways of thinking about the lesson unit and thereby allow students to draw on their previous knowledge and experience as a reference point. For example, the basic KWL strategy—what do you *know*, what do you *want* to know, and what did you *learn*—can be effectively used to help challenge gifted students. Essentially, gifted students may learn well under this constructivist teaching and motivational approach. In essence, gifted students are often motivated through learning and motivational strategies that promote discovery and reinforce of students' high intellectual capabilities. Teachers must recognize the students' special talents and focus on the motivational strategies that promote their enthusiasm for learning. Some typical motivational strategies include accelerating the learning pace, use of self-reflection, investigation and inquiry, engaging instruction, independent learning activities, and use of heuristic learning methods.

MOTIVATING STUDENTS WITH LANGUAGE BARRIERS

Teaching and motivating students with language barriers presents a twofold problem. One, the teacher needs to be concerned with teaching the learning content and helping the students learn the dominant language (i.e., English). Students with language barriers are typically referred to as ESL (English as a second language) students. Although there are other disabilities that create barriers for students to learn based on language deficits, ESL represents one of the larger groups. Therefore, the challenge for teachers is to ensure that students are progressing sufficiently so that they do not become unmotivated.

Structuring learning activities that reinforce motivation and achievement is a fundamental philosophy in motivating these types of students. For example, the use of repetition can be an effective strategy. Here, the teacher may use one word consistently, and he or she may need to repeat the word to ensure that the students grasp the meaning. This can help the students learn the language, as well as the meaning behind the word. Teachers must develop significant patience with these students and maintain a positive attitude that can be transmitted to the students themselves. Providing low-stress environments can be effective in encouraging language-deficient students to be motivated to learn. Some strategies for motivating students with language barriers include the following:

- Use visual aides to reinforce instruction.
- Structure the pace to accommodate language deficiency.
- Use selective English words with universal meaning.
- Use multiple intelligences to tailor to special needs.
- Use physical examples and exercises.
- Incorporate collaborative learning exercises.
- Use engaging exercises to maintain attention.
- Use combination of extrinsic and intrinsic rewards.
- Give praise for language achievements.
- Use multimedia and technology to support language.
- Encourage students to communicate in English.
- Use paraphrasing to reinforce performance with praise.

The use of visual aids can significantly reinforce instruction, given that students will not only hear the words but also view them. Another technique is to simply use English words that have universal meanings. Teachers should avoid jargon. Use of technology can help students, given that the student can work at his or her own pace and that several types of media can be employed. Presenting learning activities in a slow and methodical fashion can help ensure that language-deficient students grasp the material. These students generally need more time than do traditional students. The use of paraphrasing techniques can also reinforce a student's performance and ensure understanding. As with all students, the use of praise and positive reinforcement can motivate as well.

Teachers should also recognize that language-deficient students are not the same as learning-disabled students. Too often, teachers may be tempted to label these students as underachievers, which can then contribute to demotivating the students. Therefore, other techniques that may be useful may include giving students special opportunities that relate to their individual interests and abilities, giving special attention to activities that foster a positive self-concept, providing empathetic and supporting relationships to reduce potential fear and frustration, and selection of materials that are free from stereotypes (i.e., those that label them as language deficient).

MOTIVATING STUDENTS WITH LOW SELF-ESTEEM

Encountering students with low self-esteem presents a difficult situation. These students may appear to be apathetic and disinterested in learning and can frustrate even the best teachers. There are many reasons why students encounter low self-esteem. These students may sometimes be referred to as *at-risk students*. Characteristics of at-risk students may include being from a single-parent family, living in a low-income household, having dysfunctional parents who provide little praise and reinforcement, or having parents for whom the child can never live up to expectations. Many of these students have a high potential for failure unless the teacher can motivate them to excel. Some strategies for motivating students with low self-esteem include the following:

- Give significant praise and positive reinforcement.
- Encourage students to take initiative for learning.
- Build the students' self-confidence.
- Provide regular feedback for achievements.
- Use personal counseling sessions to reward efforts.
- Incorporate collaborative learning exercises.
- Use exercises that foster positive self-esteem.
- Use a combination of extrinsic and intrinsic rewards.
- Give certificates, gold stars, and tangible rewards.
- Use nonrisk exercises that limit failure.
- Encourage students to establish personal goals.
- Encourage self-expression followed by praise.

Without a doubt, one of the most important techniques to use for low self-esteem students is that of high praise and positive reinforcement. This may be the first step needed to engage the student and establish a positive teacher–student relationship. Once this relationship is established, then the teacher may employ a number of techniques, one of which can be basic humor. Humor can be a motivational technique for all students but especially for those with low self-esteem. If the student can become engaged with the learning material through fun and laughter, then the student may be reinforced to continue to learn and in turn build his or her self-esteem.

Introducing nonrisk exercises that limit failure can also benefit the students. These students cannot afford to experience failure, or it may reinforce a negative self-esteem. Therefore, the more that these students can achieve, the more they will be reinforced. As students begin to experience achievement and, hopefully, increased motivation, the teacher might encourage self-expression, through continued use of praise. Providing regular feedback for achievements, as well as personal counseling, can offer rewards as well. Ultimately, providing warm and supportive encouragement can be critical for building self-confidence for low-self-esteem students.

8

101 Ways to Motivate Students

TANGIBLE REWARD STRATEGIES

1. Letters and Certificates of Recognition

People like gifts, and so do students. Reward your students by offering tangible gifts for their good performance or behavior, to help motivate and engage them. For example, give personal letters of recognition to students who complete their homework accurately and on time. Letters of recognition can easily be done by creating a template on word-processing software and then simply typing in the student's name. Appreciation letters can be tailored to recognize different categories of achievement, such as extra initiative, creativity and originality, thoroughness, neatness, outstanding work, and significant improvement. Students can also use these awards to build their self-esteem. Increased self-esteem can help students to feel appreciated, which can result in increased engagement and motivation. Students can also be encouraged to develop a portfolio of awards and letters of recognition. The portfolio can act as an incentive to seek more rewards. Certificates of achievement can also be good expressions of appreciation. Certificates can easily be printed on most word-processing software. As with letters of appreciation, categories of achievement can also be created, such as academic excellence, attendance, good behavior, best attitude, teamwork, and exceptional effort.

2. Merchandise, Apparel, and Trophies

Besides certificates, why not try other motivational tokens of achievement, such as merchandise. Items include buttons, sports bottles, customized pencils, candy, badges, custom bookmarkers, pins, and charms. For example, you might try individual and team tokens. Each time that a student of a team excels in an area, you can reward the student or team with a token (medal or metal-plated coin). After a specific number of tokens are obtained, the student can redeem them for a prize, such as a free lunch, soft drink, or pass to a sports event. For high school students, a special parking pass can be awarded, allowing the student to park his or her car in a premium parking spot for 1 week.

If you want to keep costs down, purchase your own embosser and customize your own emblems and seals. You can create your own graphics using your school mascot and symbols that can be embossed on letters, certificates, tokens, and ribbons. Don't be afraid to be creative. Talk to your students and they can give you ideas about what motivates them and the kinds of awards that they prefer.

3. Food, Treats, and Parties

The use of extrinsic factors such as food and treats can be very motivating for students. You might include food in your class activities. For example, if you are teaching a lesson in mathematics, you can distribute a pack of raisins to all the students and then incorporate the exercise using the raisins to illustrate a mathematical point. Each student can count the total number of raisins in his or her pack, and then all the students can determine the mean, mode, and median measures of central tendency. They can also plot distributions using the raisins and, after they are finished, have a nice treat as a reward. Parties can also be motivational as a reward for team behavior after finishing extensive learning exercises. Bringing in balloons and treats along with music can be motivational as a celebration for good performance. Why not try attaching a piece of candy when distributing papers back to students who have performed well. You can also label each party with a theme, such as Hawaiian Day or other ethnic holiday. In this way students can dress up in their favorite costumes, which can add positive relationships and excitement to the classroom.

4. Contests, Grades, and Academic Awards

Why not incorporate contests within the classroom and then reward individuals or teams with appropriate grades or other academic awards. For example, the traditional spelling bee contest is a remarkable way for students to be challenged and have constructive competition. The spelling bee contests can be held with teams to reinforce collaboration. Besides spelling contests, a number of mathematics and science contests can be done. Rewarding students with good grades can be a real motivator for students for these contests. At the end of contests, don't be afraid to give team recognition and follow it up with personal recognition for students who contributed above and beyond. Although it is important to recognize team effort, individuals who contribute more should be rewarded. This helps motivate individuals to perform within the team.

5. Gold Stars and Stickers

The thought of giving gold stars and stickers to high school students may seem childish, but you might be surprised by how many students of all age levels appreciate the silliness of these rewards. If a student performs well on a test, it takes only a few seconds to put a gold star next to the student's name. When the student receives the test back, the gold star can help bring a smile to the student's face. There are a number of different stickers and stars that can be used, such as positive teamwork, apple rewards, funny faces, thank you, wow slogans, you rock! and you are the best! as well as a number of creative ideas that merchandisers have developed. However, be careful not to overuse these extrinsic rewards, or students will take them for granted and/or may view them as being too childish.

6. Educational Gifts and Puzzle Blocks

One of the more interesting motivational gifts that can be incorporated into learning is the use of puzzle blocks. The puzzle block consists of a series of five or six individual puzzle pieces that can be given to a student one at a time for completion of a certain level of performance. Once all the puzzle pieces are obtained, they form a complete picture. For example, the first puzzle piece can be a white belt, the second a green belt, and the third a black belt. Completion of all three pieces allows the student to be called a black belt, which can be displayed on the student's desk or hung on a wall. Besides using the traditional karate belts, a driver's license can be used. For example, when a student starts an assignment, he or she can be issued a driver's permit (Level 1). Then, when the student reaches Level 2, he or she can be given a puzzle piece stating "restricted driver's license." The third can be a "driver's license" and the final level a "chauffeur's license." This complete driver's license can be in the form of a ticket, which the student could then display. There are many different ideas in using plaques and puzzle blocks to motivate students. Besides these items, any type of educational gift can motivate students.

7. Self-Development Rewards

Self-development rewards include such items as tickets for an event, field trip, or conference. A student or team of students who achieve good performance can be rewarded by receiving free passes to a social event or business establishment. For example, it is common for local businesses such as pizza stores to offer free tokens that can be used for receipt of a free or low-cost pizza as a reward for self-development activities. A common idea is to reward the student for reading a prescribed number of books. A special student might also accompany a teacher to a workshop or to a local sports event. The personal attention can be motivating for the student, and the teacher may gain a lot of satisfaction as well.

INTANGIBLE REWARD STRATEGIES

8. Verbal Appreciation

Perhaps there is not a more powerful or popular technique than verbal appreciation. Teachers have long recognized the importance of providing positive verbal reinforcement for students. The simple use of verbal appreciation, when presented in a meaningful way, can be more meaningful than a tangible reward. For example, there are many expressions that can be used to motivate a student. One of the more effective expressions can simply be "You are a special student." Stating that a student is special and then pointing out some of his or her special qualities can be enriching for the student. In addition, the teacher might provide verbal appreciation and then give suggestions to the student regarding career aspirations. For example, the teacher might say that the student is a gifted individual and should consider obtaining a college degree.

9. Motivational Surveys

An interesting technique that you can employ is the use of motivational surveys. You can actually create and administer a motivational survey to your students. The survey might consist of a series of questions that ask the students to rank the items that motivate them. Some of the items on the survey might include tangible rewards, use of praise, engaging learning activities, certificates, and so on. Once the survey is administered, the teacher can compile the results and then develop actions to help address the student motivational needs. For example, if a team of students decide that the most powerful motivator is a certificate, then you can accommodate them by issuing a certificate versus assuming that some other type of reward is more important to them. The use of the survey can provide recognition for student activities and reinforce their positive behavior.

10. Enrichment Interventions

Another method of rewarding students is the use of enrichment interventions. For example, you may provide as a reward to your elementary students an enriching exercise of photography, allowing the students to take various pictures around the school building and then actually develop them digitally. Also, you might provide a special art review for the students or bring in a guest speaker to talk on an intriguing topic. For high school teachers, one idea for science students can be to schedule a trip to a medical facility and allow the students to dissect a cadaver. This enriching exercise can be motivational for students and can inspire them to pursue careers in science and biology.

11. Social Needs

One of the most powerful motivators for students is their peer group. Students often compare their own performance with other students.

Especially at the teenage level, students care about what other students feel about them. Therefore, you can utilize the intangible strategy of helping to meet social needs of students through team exercises. For example, you may conduct a team-building exercise where the students work together to accomplish a task. This team exercise can include simulating survival in the desert and ranking the items most valuable for their survival. These types of activities can provide a social connection for the students in gaining interpersonal skills and contributing to positive relationships.

12. Good Character Traits

Don't be afraid to reward students for good character traits. The expression that "a good student is also a good person" is important for developing the moral infrastructure of a person. Personal characteristics such as responsibility, generosity, self-discipline, hard work, altruism, and sensitivity and care to fellow students can positively affect the learning environment and motivate students. Recognizing these traits in students and valuing these character traits can be motivational. You can positively influence the students' character development by recognizing good qualities, such as respect, justice, honesty, and responsibility in students. Developing these positive character traits may have a direct correlation in helping students achieve.

13. Individual Values

Your ability as a teacher to recognize some of the values that are important to a student can be motivational. For example, if a student places a high value on his or her family, church, peer group, or athletic coach, recognizing these values and then showing appreciation to these people for the student performance can be motivational. For example, if a student is participating in a sport and he or she performs well in the classroom, you can send a letter or verbally recognize the student's performance to his or her coach, and the student can then gain great satisfaction from this gesture. Gaining recognition from a teacher or a coach can serve to foster additional positive behavior or academic performance.

14. Coaching Strategies

Providing good coaching to a student can be powerful in helping students recognize their areas in need of improvement and to reinforce positive behaviors. You can act as a mentor in describing areas in which the student can improve and showing real concern for the student as a person. This special attention through a coaching session can help the student to recognize areas to improve, and it can help to provide motivation for the student to excel.

15. Ignore Trivial Misbehavior

It may be effective in certain instances for you to ignore trivial misbehavior. You must use good judgment in deciding when to nip the problem in the bud or ignore the behavior. Sometimes, students may use trivial misbehavior to gain attention from you. In this instant you may want to recognize that the student is only seeking attention and the teacher may provide positive reinforcement for the student. However, be careful with this technique so that the behavior is not reinforced and the misbehavior escalates.

16. Engaging Activities

Providing engaging activities can be an intangible strategy to help motivate students. The traditional technique of a KWL chart (*What do you know? What do you want to know?* and *What have you learned?*) can be a strategy of helping to engage students in brainstorming ideas, working together cooperatively, exchanging ideas, problem solving and decision making, and teamwork. There are a number of different engaging strategies that teachers can use to help motivate their students, such as discovering what is available within the school neighborhood and making use of these resources. Perhaps your school is located next to a business, and you can provide an engaging activity by showing real-life experiences for the students. The students can then demonstrate their understanding of the business through simulated classroom activities.

17. Nonverbal Messages

The use of nonverbal communication, or body language, is a technique that can be easily employed by teachers. For example, the use of facial expressions and eye contact can greatly influence your perception and feelings toward students. Showing facial expressions of concern and appreciation versus anger and frustration can send vivid signals to students and affect their motivation. While listening to the student, providing good eye contact is critical. The science of nonverbal communication involves kinesics. Kinesics involves movement of the body, and you should be aware of the impact of these movements on the student. For example, if you cross your arms and create blockage between you and the student, this may send negative signals to the student, and, as a result, the student may become less motivated. Therefore, being aware of nonverbal messages and providing openness can be helpful. While listening to students, it is important to refrain from irritating listening habits, such as pacing back and forth, never smiling, doodling, working on something else, or providing an expression of a poker face. Always be aware of your nonverbals and their impact on students.

18. Adapting to Student's Style

Have you ever wondered why it's easier to talk to some students than others? At times you may feel that students are talking on a different wavelength or that they are simply not communicating at all. You can feel the frustration and bewilderment of failed communication. The ability to speak the language of your students is important not only for effective communication but in building relationships. Miscommunication can be avoided, or at least minimized, if you attempt to identify the dominant personality style of the student and then adapt your style to his or hers. For example, based on the work of the famous psychoanalyst Carl Jung, four primary personality styles are the intuitor, feeler, thinker, and doer. Recognizing the style of the student can be helpful in communicating and, in turn, providing incentive for the student. For example, be enthusiastic and stimulating when talking to the intuitor. For the feeler, try to personalize discussion and be concerned about feelings and individuality. Present ideas in an organized and structured manner for the thinker. Give alternatives and don't push for immediate action. For the doer, get to the point. Try to be practical, spirited, and down to earth. For example, if your style is a thinker and you are dealing with a student who is an intuitor, you may come across as being too structured, overly cautious, and conservative. You may believe that the student rambles in a conceptual manner, is hard to pin down, and is too spontaneous and nonconforming. Therefore, the key to improving communication and working relationships with students is your ability to adapt your style to the student and the situation. This can be called *style flexing*. After all, the road to effective communication and motivation starts with communication, and the best way to communicate is to start by speaking the language of your students.

19. Allow the Student to Save Face

You should always try and let the student save face. Students generally have high peer identification, and any embarrassment in front of students' peers can be devastating to their self-esteem. This, in turn, can demotivate students. Not only is it potentially damaging for a teacher to discipline a student in front of his or her peers, but it can also have a negative impact on the class as a whole. When students see a student being disciplined in front of the class, they may also feel as if they are being reprimanded.

FORMAL REWARD STRATEGIES

20. Scholastic Reward

The scholastic reward is a powerful motivator in which you provide avenues for the student to achieve special recognition by an organization. For example, encouraging a student for good performance to become a National Merit Scholar can be very motivational. Other formal scholastic rewards may consist of National Honor Society, High Honor Roll, AP Scholar, National Society of Scholars, International Society for Philosophical Enquiry, and Who's Who Among American Students. Achieving these scholastic honors can be motivational for the student, and making these awards available is the responsibility of the teacher.

21. Contests and Competition Rewards

Students are often motivated by competition. Many students thrive on the opportunity to participate in competition to demonstrate their proficiency or unique abilities. Special contests may include subject-specific contests, games, and sports events. Some of these contests might also generate special recognition, such as most improved award, best team player, or actual academic success award.

22. Volunteer Activities

Volunteer activities can be motivational for students by giving them recognition and helping them building character. Examples of volunteer activities for students may include working with buddy-baseball (baseball league for special-needs children), Public Action to Deliver Shelter (PADS—providing services for local homeless people), soup kitchens, a local leukemia or cancer society, construction projects, or cleaning efforts. These activities can indirectly help motivate students to feel more connected with their school. For example, if a student is learning a language such as Spanish and is involved with a Spanish club, the teacher may arrange an activity whereby students can provide assistance, such as at a local homeless shelter, serving food to Spanish-speaking people. This event in itself can be motivational because the student can practice his or her Spanish and at the same time provide a goodwill volunteer activity for the needy.

23. Special Events and Guest Speakers

Hosting special events at a school or using guest speakers to enrich the classroom can break the doldrums of the traditional classroom. For example, if the class topic involves science, bringing in an orthopedic surgeon and demonstrating how to repair a broken leg by putting a cast on a student's leg can be very enriching. The surgeon can explain the concept of a fracture and then actually put a cast on a student's leg and allow the students to sign their autographs on the cast. This activity can be fun and educational. At the completion of the exercise, the surgeon can demonstrate the removal of a cast by cutting the cast off and then allowing the student to keep the cast as a souvenir. Another idea of a special event can be to bring in a local drama or theater group. This group can demonstrate in a theatrical way a concept that the students are currently learning in the classroom.

24. Community Recognition

Allowing involvement of students in community events can provide a rewarding experience for them and also a valuable service for the community. For example, students may become involved in raising money for a local war veteran who is in need of medical treatment or care. For example, one school provided a fund-raising activity for a soldier who was paralyzed in the Iraq War. The students collected money, and then several students paid a visit to the veteran, which was photographed and reported in the local newspaper. These kinds of community events can contribute to a common good for all.

25. Administrator Recognition

Never overlook the importance of asking an administrator such as a principal, assistant principal, or dean to provide a letter of recognition for a student's exceptional performance or behavior. Administrators are often viewed highly by students, and to receive verbal recognition or a letter is motivational.

26. Board of Education Recognition

As with the administrator, you can take advantage of the Board of Education by requesting that students be placed on the agenda at a board meeting so that they can be recognized for their outstanding performance. You may allow students to provide a description of their accomplishment and then allow the board members to ask questions. If students completed a project, the student may demonstrate the project to the board members, which can benefit the board members in seeing results of a student's performance.

27. Mayor of the City Award

As with community recognition, you should not hesitate to ask that the local mayor of the city recognize students for outstanding performance.

Many towns and cities have a special Mayor's Recognition Award for outstanding citizens. These awards are often given to students of the community for special achievements that involve the community. Receiving an award from the mayor can also encourage students to pursue their career or higher education aspirations. The award can bring recognition not only to the student and school but also to the entire student body, which can be motivational for other students as well.

LEADERSHIP STRATEGIES

28. Be Responsive

A famous race car driver once was asked, "What is the key to success in the race car business?" He thought for a moment and then replied, "If you are in total control of your driving all the time, you aren't driving fast enough." What he was saying was that you have to be on the edge. This doesn't mean that you are to be reckless, but you, as an educator, need to be on the cutting edge and stay current with new instructional ideas, or other educators are going to pass you by. Therefore, by remaining current (being responsive to students' needs), your students will recognize your efforts, and the result will be that your students will be more motivated in class. For example, if you are lacking in technology skills and many of your students are proficient, you will lose respect and may experience difficulty in relating and instructing to your students.

29. Quality and Professionalism

There is a quality expression that states, "If you go on board a bus and you know that the seats are dirty, start worrying about the engines." Quality and professionalism are important to motivate students. A teacher who presents himself or herself unprofessionally or is unclean may demotivate his or her students, and they, in turn, may worry about the quality of instruction. Students often adapt behaviors of their role models. Therefore, always providing quality educational materials, appearance, and dress can be motivational for all.

30. Serve Your Customer

Serving your customer (the student) entails meeting or exceeding the expectations for learning. One way to be responsive to students' immediate needs is using the four-by-four rule. You should be within four feet of each of your students every four minutes. This simple idea can help you to be available for your students' immediate needs. Students who have questions—especially, those who are eager to obtain your attention—need to have timely feedback, or they may become discouraged.

31. Collaboration

There once was an experiment where a teacher asked the students to work individually in solving a problem within a given time limit. While solving the problem, the teacher noticed that students became frustrated because the teacher had imposed a deadline and they were concerned that some students were performing better than they were. The teacher then allowed the students to work in teams and gave the same time limit, but this time the students experienced less stress and were motivated to perform. Therefore, the use of teamwork and collaboration can often help break down stress and individual competition.

32. Be Proactive

The job of the educator can be a difficult one, and it requires an enormous amount of energy in attending to students' needs. You need to be proactive and anticipate students' needs; otherwise, they may become demotivated. For example, if students are interested in playing guitar (assuming that you play guitar) you might form an after-school guitar class. This class can help the students feel socially connected to teacher, classmates, and school.

33. Be Open-Minded

Students come to classrooms with a variety of backgrounds and interests. Your ability to be open-minded and appreciate the different interests of students can help in connecting with them. For example, some students may enjoy rap music whereas other students may have a passion for a sport. The ability for you to at least understand and be aware of different types of music and sports can help in connecting with the student.

34. Respect Diversity

Students have a multiplicity of ethnic backgrounds, which can range from Hispanic, African American, Asian, Caucasian, and so on. Respecting diversity and encouraging the celebration of various ethnic traditions can help to motivate students and provide a deep relationship between you and the student. For example, you may allow all the students in a classroom to celebrate each of the special traditions, such as Kwanzaa for African American students.

35. Passion and Commitment

There is an old expression in negotiating that one of the characteristics of a successful negotiator is his or her ability to gain power, which can be done through the person's commitment and passion to the negotiation process. A person who believes in what he or she does will acquire more power, which will allow him or her to be more effective in his or her role. The teacher who demonstrates commitment and passion for his or her work will foster this in his or her students as well.

36. Continual Improvement

There is a traditional expression, "If it ain't broke, don't fix it." This expression has been criticized by many modern educators as lacking continual improvement. The new expression may be "If you care about it, continually improve it so that it doesn't break down." Continual improvement involves being an effective leader and constantly providing improved learning strategies for students.

37. Change Your Paradigm

The expression "It ain't what you don't know; it's what you know that ain't so" can be appropriate for motivating students. In the business world, people know the importance of changing their paradigms (how they see their business products), so that they can remain competitive. For example, for years engineers were attempting to build a better carburetor on a car, until one engineer discovered that the new paradigm "is not to build a better carburetor but to be able to get the fuel mixture in the cylinders." So, with this change of paradigm, the invention of fuel injection was created. Therefore, changing your paradigm regarding how students are educated can be helpful in providing new learning strategies.

38. Self-Fulfilling Prophecy

The theory of the self-fulfilling prophecy, often called the *Pygmalion effect*, is a powerful theory of human motivation. The theory suggests that a belief or expectation in an event can actually cause it to happen. Therefore, if you expect positive behavior from a student, this expectation can greatly influence a student to behave properly. Likewise, if you establish high expectations for student performance, chances are that the student will aspire to meet those expectations.

39. Moral Leadership

Maintaining high ethics, a servant attitude, and high moral leadership can be effective in reaching students. Moral leadership involves the characteristic of meeting the diverse needs of students in an organization. The concept of moral leadership entails the view of providing value-added education. The primary goal, therefore, of moral leadership is to serve the needs of students. By providing moral leadership, students will recognize and develop a better attitude themselves.

DISCIPLINE STRATEGIES

40. Understand Defense Mechanisms

Students often resort to using defense mechanisms to protect themselves from experiencing bad feelings. For example, if a student anticipates doing poorly on a test, the student may use avoidance as a defense mechanism.

Avoidance may entail not studying or becoming sick to prevent taking the test and having the resulting bad feelings. Students may also deny that they are doing poorly in school as a defense mechanism of not accepting the reality of poor performance. You need to be able to understand these defense mechanisms and how they can give you clues to what the student is really thinking. If a student resorts to the defense mechanism of avoidance or denial, you can pick up on the cues and respond accordingly.

41. Understanding Human Needs

Students, like all people, have common human needs. For example, one need is to feel socially connected with fellow students. Therefore, establishing programs that can promote self-esteem and peer recognition can be useful in motivating students. Using the program of peer mediation to help resolve disciplinary problems can be an effective motivator. Rather than a teacher resolving conflict among students, the students themselves can work with a trained peer in mediating their differences. The premise of peer mediation is to allow students to negotiate and work out their differences by themselves rather than through a higher authority. When students are able to work out their differences among themselves, they may be more apt to accept responsibility for the behavior, resolve the conflict, and be more motivated for good behavior in the classroom.

42. Rules of Behavior

Establishing clear-cut rules of behavior in the classroom is the foundation for good classroom management and motivation. When establishing rules, it is important to make the rules in a positive manner. Instead of saying "Don't run in the halls," state "Please walk in the halls." The use of positive behavior can contribute to students' taking on more responsibility for motivating their own behavior.

43. Emotional Intelligence

Emotions play a fundamental part in communicating with students. Your ability to recognize your own level of emotional intelligence and to understand the impact of the emotions can directly contribute to the students' own behavior. For example, knowing what feelings are triggered and what sets you off as a teacher is important in maintaining control and self-regulation. Moreover, understanding empathy and building effective relationships through positive feedback and constructive criticism can improve your ability to cope with stressful situations.

44. Punishment

The use of punishment may be the main reason for taking disciplinary action against a student. Although punishment should not be the prime reason for disciplining a student, it may be necessary in rare or extreme cases as a wake-up call for the student in understanding the severe gravity of a behavior and to help motivate the student for good behavior.

45. Progressive Action

The process of taking disciplinary action to motivate a student should be taken from the standpoint of being corrective, not punitive. The model of progressive discipline is the best way of dealing with students, with due process, fairness, and a way in which extenuating circumstances can be considered. Essentially, the goal of progressive discipline is to give the student opportunity for self-correction before taking more serious measures. Progressive discipline attempts to improve students' behavior for the future rather than punish the student by focusing on the past. You should take progressive measures, such as talking with the student, issuing a verbal or written warning, or giving a suspension.

46. Discipline Styles

When you manage disciplinary problems in the classroom, you develop a discipline style. Discipline styles are based on the degrees of your enforcing rules and supporting students. You may take a style of being a supporter, negotiator, compromiser, abdicator, or enforcer. Try using a variety of different styles to get the best results. Try not to rely on one style only, such as enforcing rules consistently, as opposed to considering other styles as well.

47. Discipline by Negotiations

The negotiator is a teacher who places great value on a win-win approach to disciplining students (i.e., discipline by negotiations). Don't think of negotiating with students as being negative. A negotiator's objective is to obtain results, and listening to the students' needs and motives behind disciplinary behaviors can be valuable in demonstrating respect and care for the student.

48. Tactics and Countertactics

When you are confronted with tactics by students, you are forced to rely on your own arsenal of countertactics. Becoming proficient in dealing with various tactics that a student may employ, such as the emotional tantrum, can be useful for you in correcting behavior. For example, a countertactic to an emotional tantrum may be to ignore the tactic or confront the emotionalism and focus on the facts.

49. Establish a Vision

The first step in implementing a good disciplinary program is to establish a vision for success. The vision should include the rules and conduct, and it should be communicated to all the students. The vision plan serves as a foundation for the ongoing process and helps to maintain a precise picture of the desired outcomes. The vision can also help to motivate, overcome roadblocks, and provide resources for encountering disciplinary problems.

50. Establishing Good Policies

The foundation to motivating students for good behavior is to first establish good disciplinary policies. You should periodically review your policies, as compared to other schools' disciplinary policies, and, when necessary, adapt the best policies that are most suitable for your own school.

51. Good Time Management

Do you ever feel overwhelmed with too many things coming at you in the classroom? Learning to manage your time is much like trying to stick to a diet or stop smoking: To be successful, you must first have a genuine desire and commitment to improve. Learning to manage your time can significantly help in reducing discipline problems (i.e., disorganization leads to student misbehavior). Poor time management can result in demotivating students because they will become confused and generally recognize the inefficiency. Employing some simple techniques, such as making a daily to-do list, prioritizing your activities, eliminating time wasters, delegating activities, classifying similar activities, and maximizing every minute of the day, can be a start in obtaining good time management skills.

COMMUNICATION STRATEGIES

52. Be Straight With Students

When you play mind games and manipulate your students through the use of double-talk, this action only reinforces a classroom environment that encourages misbehavior. Mind games can be any type of interaction among people who have ulterior motives instead of being honest and straightforward. Therefore, it is important that you always talk honestly (straight) with your students.

53. Avoid Scolding Students

When you become stressed and overly emotional with students, it is easy to resort to scolding. If scolded on a continual basis, students will become immune to this practice and will shut down. Students become disrespectful and demotivated toward teachers who scold them. Apathy and low self-esteem can result. Remember to stay positive and avoid scolding your students.

54. Provide Realistic Expectations

When communicating to students, provide realistic expectations for students' performance. When you provide unreasonable goals or expectations, students become demotivated and view the goals as futile. Beliefs become reality. Therefore, always provide positive expectations, challenging goals, and realistic expectations.

55. Provide Two-Way Communication

When talking with students, try to avoid one-way communication (i.e., you do all the talking to the student). Two-way communication (both parties sharing discussion) can foster respect and motivation by allowing you to understand the student's perspective and, at the same time, allowing yourself to express your opinions.

56. Use Paraphrasing

The method of paraphrasing involves restating in your own words what the student has communicated to you. Paraphrasing helps to verify understanding of the message, and it demonstrates good active listening and respect toward the student.

57. Use Restatement

The technique of restatement is useful in addressing statements that are confusing, and there is a need to clarify your understanding of the information. When students attempt to explain their thoughts, they may not always express them well. Therefore, restatement entices the student to talk more on the subject. For example, if a student states that he or she feels sad today, you simply can respond, "You feel sad today?" This response will help encourage the student to clarify the message.

58. Use Close-Ended Questions

Another technique that can help to motivate students and foster good communication is the use of close-ended questions. Close-ended questions require a simple yes-or-no answer. This technique can be useful when time is a factor and a yes-or-no answer is best. However, be careful in using this technique so that you don't come across as too abrupt or impatient to the student.

59. Use Expanders

The use of reinforcing gestures and statements, such as "Go on," "I see," and "Uh-huh," encourages the student to continue talking and helps the student to recognize that you are truly listening to him or her. These statements, called *expanders*, can help the student feel more comfortable in talking with you.

60. Use Silence

Surprisingly, one of the best ways that you can communicate with students is through silence. This technique works on the premise that when a person is faced with silence, he or she usually talks. Also, it allows time for the student to present his or her ideas without interruption. Therefore, consider promoting communications with students by using this technique, and you may find some increased motivation as well.

61. Be Patient

You can improve your success with students by developing the virtue of patience. Exhibiting patience can be effective in dealing with misbehavior, too. For example, if a student misbehaves, you might ask the student to step out in the hall or the back of the room for a few moments as an excuse to give time for the student to contemplate his or her behavior. You need to be careful not to embarrass or humiliate the student. Although every situation calls for good judgment, selecting the most appropriate approach, such as patience, can be key to resolving misbehavior and adding to motivation.

62. Active Listening

Listening goes way beyond hearing. An active listener is one who is able to process information and then communicate back to the speaker. Your ability to actively listen to students recognize their feelings, emotions, and actual content of the interaction is important in establishing motivation and a positive relationship with the student.

STRESS MANAGEMENT STRATEGIES

63. Understanding Your Tolerance

Three sources of stress for any individual—to say the least, a teacher—are those that are physical, mental, and emotional. The ability to understand which of these sources is causing you stress and then utilizing another source can reduce your stress. For example, if you are emotionally at your limit, you may want to physically exercise to reduce your overall stress. Understanding stress management techniques and your tolerance can be important in establishing a productive classroom environment.

64. Practice Self-Talk

People often talk to themselves (i.e., practice self-talk), and this can be negative or positive. Negative self-talk can be described as dwelling on negative thoughts. However, using positive self-talk (concentrating on positive thoughts) can reduce your stress. This technique can also be used with students to help motivate them. Explaining this technique to your students and encouraging them to use positive self-talk can help reduce their stress and develop a more positive attitude.

65. Enjoy the Moment

Learn to enjoy the moment at any given time. Don't live for tomorrow. Too often, teachers who become dissatisfied with the profession focus too much on only the end of the school day. However, this can produce negative cues to students, and, as a result, they can become demotivated. Learning to enjoy the moment can help you develop positive feelings that can in turn transfer to your students.

66. Understand Your Vulnerability

Another concept of creating a motivational environment for students lies in understanding your own personal vulnerability to the context you are placed in. People in any given situation will have different degrees of vulnerability (e.g., high or low vulnerability). If you have high vulnerability, the result will be higher stress, and you'll probably be less effective in motivating students and maintaining a positive environment. For example, if your students are causing stress in you, recognizing your vulnerability and then employing effective stress management techniques can be the first step in managing stress.

67. Set Realistic Goals

One cause of stress in students may be when teachers place too high academic aspirations on them. Unrealistic goals imposed by teachers can produce stress in both students and yourself. Therefore, set realistic goals for academic achievement, and students will be more likely to be motivated.

68. Externalize Your Situation

People either internalize or externalize situations in their lives. When you internalize your feelings about a situation, this can cause increased stress. For example, if students are experiencing difficulties at home because of violence or financial hardship, overly internalizing these feelings can actually make you less effective. Consider externalizing these feelings and looking at the situation more objectively; you may be more effective in dealing with these difficult situations and in turn experience less stress.

69. Find a Useful Context

As an educator, you will experience many disappointments. And, although it may be appropriate to sulk, don't sulk too long. Learn to get over it. For example, if you mishandle a situation with a student, reflect on this experience (what you did well and not so well) and grow from the experience. In other words there often can be some ultimate positive result from the experience (a useful context). Often, these disappointing experiences result in growth and learning for you, and, in turn, you can find new ways to motivate your students. So, look for the positives in these experiences and develop new strategies for improvement.

70. Don't Be a Typhoid Mary

The classic story of Typhoid Mary depicts a waitress who was a typhoid carrier and infected many people, who became sick and died, but she was fine. Much like Typhoid Mary, don't become a stress carrier and impose a lot of stress on students. Although you feel fine, the students may become stressed and demotivated.

71. Use Positive Visualization

When a person becomes stressed, one of the techniques that can be used is positive visualization. Picture yourself on a pleasant environment, such as a beach or other relaxing spot. This technique can also be helpful for students when they are experiencing stress. Encourage students to think positively versus negatively. Much like when a person has experienced a nightmare and breaks out in a cold sweat, the nightmare itself is not actually happening, but the mind perceives it as really happening and the body reacts accordingly. Therefore, thinking negative thoughts can cause stress on the body. The notion of positive visualization is to think positive thoughts, and the body, in turn, will be less stressful.

72. Think Stop

When experiencing stress, use the *think stop* technique to prevent negative self-talk. Picture a bright red stop sign and stop dwelling on negative self-talk. Slowly shift negative thoughts to positive thoughts. This technique can be used by all educators and students.

CLASS MANAGEMENT STRATEGIES

73. Drive Out Fear

Students have a difficult time functioning in a classroom environment of fear. The ability to drive out fear so that students feel free to express their thoughts in a productive manner can help motivate the student.

74. Organize Your Classroom

Critical to establishing motivation for students is identifying the most appropriate learning environment in a classroom setting by organizing your classroom. Effectively arranging your educational resources in a productive learning environment can help motivate students for good behavior and performance.

75. Motivational Planning

Teachers often prepare good lesson plans but don't always incorporate good motivational techniques within the plan. Don't hesitate to examine the special needs of your students and incorporate activities that help engage and stimulate them. Provide positive environmental conditions, such as appropriate control of lighting, ventilation, and temperature, which can affect the learning environment. Be aware of your environment and provide the best conditions to motivate your students.

76. Positive Use of Wall Space

Don't hesitate to be creative in developing a positive environment through use of bulletin boards and your wall space. Bulletin boards and wall space can be used to display student work, posters, articles of interest, and other information to help motivate students.

77. Effective Use of Floor Space

The arrangement of students' desks, the teacher's desk, bookcases, and cabinets can be critical in providing an optimum environment for students to learn and be motivated. For example, you may want to place your desk in a location in which you can best see all your students at one time. Likewise, you may want to position students' desks in the best arrangement that supports the learning exercises that you conduct in the classroom.

78. Effective Use of Storage Space

As with the classroom, make use of effective storage space by storing your educational supplies, equipment, and instructional materials in a convenient and accessible manner. This will allow you to be more productive in providing instruction in the classroom and, in turn, reduce distractions to your students.

79. Provide Necessary Safety and Security

In certain situations, it may be necessary to pay close attention to ensuring that the students feel safe and secure in the classroom. You may want to eliminate certain distractions and provide convenient positioning of resources so that students feel safe without the threat of harm from other students. You may want to provide a private area for students to study, and avoid crowding desks that hinder learning.

80. Provide Clinical Settings

You also may examine ways to provide a clinical setting for students to participate in projects and exercises, especially from a team standpoint. Instead of arranging classes in the traditional rows, you may want to obtain tables so that students can work together on projects.

81. Effective Task Management

The concept of task management involves making sure that all materials in the classroom are accessible to students and yourself. Task management involves the convenient acquisition of supplies and equipment so that students can partake in a seamless learning experience without interruptions.

82. Be Flexible

Once you have established the resources in your room, don't feel as if this arrangement is permanent. Your ability to be flexible and change the arrangement to meet new educational goals is important in motivating students. Different activities require different room arrangements.

INSTRUCTIONAL STRATEGIES

83. Good Lesson Plans

The foundation of good instructional strategy begins with a good lesson plan. Make sure that your lesson plan incorporates good objectives, description of motivational factors, materials needed, description of activities, and other resources needed.

84. Use Differentiated Instruction

The use of differentiated instruction is best defined as providing instruction that reaches all diverse students. Recognize that no two students are alike, and structure your lessons to provide the best instructional methods to differentiate among your students.

85. Incorporate Reflective Instruction

Allow time for your students to reflect on their experiences. Reflection can allow the students to examine their underlying assumptions, consciously consider their decision-making processes, and allow them to become aware of the consequences for their actions. Encourage your students to be reflective about their ethical decisions, values, and treatment of others as a means for providing good motivation.

86. Provide Authentic Assessment

There are many ways to provide assessment for students, other than traditional written examinations. Authentic assessment involves selecting the best method in which to measure performance of students, such as use of portfolios, personal observation, demonstration, role play, and behavioral skills development activities. These types of assessment can be less stressful than traditional methods for the students and help to motivate them.

87. Use Good Openings

One of the most difficult aspects of giving a lesson or presentation is the first few minutes of instruction, called the *opening*. A good opening needs to engage your students. Some examples of a good opening include creating curiosity and interest, stating the objectives, establishing goodwill with your students, providing an overview for the material to be presented, and providing a catchy attention getter.

88. Use Good Transitions

The ability to smoothly move from one point to another is called *transitioning*. Good transitions can help the teacher to move successfully from one topic to another and maintain the interest of students. Techniques to help provide effective transitions include momentarily pausing between topics, allowing for questions, summarizing the information, explaining how one topic relates to the other, and simply telling the students that you're moving to the next topic.

89. Use Effective Methods to Get Attention

An important aspect of instruction is to obtain the initial attention of students. There are many ways to gain students' attention, such as telling an opening story, telling a joke, asking for the students' attention, using a gimmick or creating a visual devise, providing a statement of impact, or stating a quotation. Gaining the students' attention can be critical in establishing the initial motivation for learning.

90. Providing Good Facilitation

Effective teachers know how to be good facilitators in the classroom versus lecturing at the chalkboard. Using good techniques of facilitation, such as incorporating role plays, behavioral modeling, synergistic exercises, simulation, and problem-solving activities, can help to facilitate learning.

91. Use Humor in Your Instruction

The use of humor can motivate students and increase their interest. Henson (2004, citing Holm, 2002) states that "numerous empirical studies have found that the use of humor in the classroom engages students in active learning, motivates interests, and increases retention" (p. 331). So, don't hesitate to tell a joke from time to time.

BUILDING RELATIONSHIP STRATEGIES

92. Begin With Hopes, Fears, and Expectations

One strategy that you can use, especially with a new class, is to begin by asking for the students' hopes, fears, and expectations for the class. The students can identify some of their hopes for learning, some of the fears they may have, and also some of the performance expectations they'd like to achieve. This can get the class off to a good start. Posting these responses on the chalkboard and then discussing them can help to establish an initial positive relationship.

93. Building Effective Teamwork

The quality of the effectiveness of learning is dependent on the ability of students to learn the subject and the quality of the relationship that they have with you. Building teamwork through establishing a productive environment and viewing the educational process as a team effort between you and the students can help in motivating both you and the students.

94. Use Concession Making

Concession making means giving up (conceding) something to obtain something in negotiations. Don't be hesitant about negotiating with a student to help ensure that the student maintains a positive self-esteem. For example, when dealing with a child with a low self-esteem, you might begin by praising the student or giving the student an extrinsic reward for good behavior or performance. Praising the student sometimes reduces conflict and can actually help the student to talk with you and be positive toward you.

95. Be Willing to Modify Expectations

Modifying the expectations for a student may be an effective technique for students who are experiencing academic difficulties. If a challenging student refuses to work, you might bargain with the student by suggesting that the student complete the work in segments or through alternative methods. For example, you might ask the student for a suggestion on how to best complete an assignment or suggest completing a portion of the assignment instead of the entire assignment. This may be better than nothing and help the student to be motivated to learn.

96. Confront Student Feelings

If a student is experiencing strong emotions of anger or frustration, his or her behavior may be manifested through open defiance. In these cases, you may need to communicate directly with the student and confront his or her feelings. You might start by asking the student how he or she is feeling about the behavior. In this way you can begin to personalize the relationship and draw out the student's reason for the behavior. Students often base their behavior on emotions that they are feeling at a given time.

97. Keep Communications Open

Keeping the lines of communications open between you and the student is important in maintaining healthy personal relationships. Students need to feel that they are respected by you and are able to talk with you without fear and humiliation. It is not uncommon for a teacher to attempt to stifle a misbehaving student by harshly criticizing the student. Although the misbehavior may stop, the student may harbor ill feelings and resentment toward you.

98. Initiate Collaborative Negotiations

It is much easier to negotiate with students from a collaborative position than from a competitive one. Collaborative negotiation is based on the notion that both parties are willing to come to agreement. Don't feel that you always have to be the dictator. Taking a team approach can create a healthy, positive environment with your students.

99. Mentor Your Students

Mentoring your students by talking with them as a coach can be effective in gaining their respect and establishing a positive relationship. There are many methods for mentoring a student. You may engage in a short discussion with the student in the classroom or a more formal discussion by asking the student to stay after school to talk. During the mentoring session, you should take time to get the facts from the student, describe the desired behavior or performance, actively listen to the student, obtain agreement for resolving an issue, and provide positive reinforcement for future performance.

100. Developing Honesty and Trust

The foundation of building positive relationships between you and your students begins with establishing core values of honesty and trust. Most business people do not want to go into a business relationship with a person whom they do not trust. Likewise, students will be reluctant to work with you if they cannot trust you. Establishing trust begins by being honest with students in your dealings with them. Honesty can help to develop trust, which takes time. Once you have established trust with your students, building their motivation can be easier.

101. Care About Students, but Be Skillful

It is important to care about students, but if teachers are not competent and skillful, chances are that students will not excel or be motivated. Newman (2006) reinforces this by stating, "Admittedly, teaching is no job for people who do not care about young people, but personal concern is not the only quality teachers need" (p. 7). Therefore, care about students, but be skillful in your teaching and leadership.

Appendix A

Teacher Motivation Styles Inventory

Directions: Indicate how often you exhibit each of the behaviors when motivating your students by placing a check in the column next to each statement according to the following scale:

A = *almost never*   S = *sometimes*   F = *frequently*   V = *very frequently*

Motivation Behavior		Frequency		
1. I am unassertive in motivating students.	A	S	F	V
2. I tend to ignore apathetic students.	A	S	F	V
3. I manipulate my students to motivate them.	A	S	F	V
4. I exhibit high control over my students.	A	S	F	V
5. I counsel my students on their lack of motivation.	A	S	F	V
6. I am indecisive in motivating students.	A	S	F	V
7. I tend to intimidate my students.	A	S	F	V
8. I try to avoid disciplining my students.	A	S	F	V
9. I can be "wishy-washy" with my students.	A	S	F	V
10. I am personal, but assertive with my students.	A	S	F	V
11. I am accommodating with my students.	A	S	F	V
12. I tend to avoid unmotivated students.	A	S	F	V
13. I tend to be a dictator with my students.	A	S	F	V
14. I tend to collaborate with my students.	A	S	F	V
15. I tend to compromise with my students.	A	S	F	V
16. I am "soother/supporter" with my students.	A	S	F	V
17. I tend to be apathetic in motivating my students.	A	S	F	V
18. I can be very assertive with my students.	A	S	F	V
19. I am inconsistent in motivating my students.	A	S	F	V
20. I take a "win-win" position with students.	A	S	F	V
21. I "look the other way" with unmotivated students.	A	S	F	V
22. I am very sensitive about students' feelings.	A	S	F	V
23. I aggressively confront apathetic students.	A	S	F	V

(continued)

Motivation Behavior		Frequency		
24. I try to find "middle ground" with my students.	A	S	F	V
25. I view motivation as a team approach.	A	S	F	V
26. I try to be helpful and gracious with students.	A	S	F	V
27. I regularly send students to the disciplinary dean.	A	S	F	V
28. I like to "give and take" with students.	A	S	F	V
29. I can be threatening to my students.	A	S	F	V
30. I talk with my students to reach a mutual result.	A	S	F	V

SCORING OF TEACHER MOTIVATION STYLES INVENTORY

Directions: Score each of the questions by giving a number for each question, using the following point system.

A = 1 point   S = 2 points   F = 3 points   V = 4 points

Write the number of points for each question on the scoring line for each of the questions. For example, if you answered Question 1 with *very frequently*, place a 4 on the line designated for Question 1. If you answered *frequently*, give yourself 3 points. If you answered *sometimes*, give yourself 2 points, and if you answered the question *almost never*, write 1 point in the designated line for Question 1.

Place a point for each of the questions on the lines, respectively. When finished, add the number for each column and put the total on the line at the bottom.

	Supporter	Abdicator	Enforcer	Compromiser	Negotiator
1.	____				
2.		____			
3.				____	
4.			____		
5.					____
6.	____				
7.			____		
8.		____			
9.				____	
10.					____
11.	____				
12.		____			
13.			____		
14.					____
15.				____	
16.	____				
17.		____			
18.			____		
19.				____	
20.					____
21.		____			

(*continued*)

	Supporter	Abdicator	Enforcer	Compromiser	Negotiator
22.	_____				
23.			_____		
24.				_____	
25.					_____
26.	_____				
27.		_____			
28.				_____	
29.		_____			
30.					_____
Total	_____	_____	_____	_____	_____

EXPLANATION OF MOTIVATION STYLES SCORING

The interpretation of the Teacher Motivation Styles Inventory can be useful for examining your strengths and weaknesses in motivating students. A high score for any given style indicates a preference for utilizing this style in motivating students. A low score indicates that you do not have a preference in using this style.

If you scored high in the *enforcer* category, it suggests that you use this style predominantly in motivating students, as compared to the other styles. If you are experiencing a great deal of motivation problems, it may be a result of utilizing this style too frequently. Excessive use of the enforcer style may be creating more motivational problems because the students may resent the overuse of this style and rebel. If you had a low score in this category and you are experiencing frequent problems, you might consider being more assertive in your motivation of students.

If you scored high in the *compromiser* category, it suggests that you tend to compromise frequently with your students. You may be viewed by students as being too inconsistent, wishy-washy, and manipulative. The compromiser style may also be viewed as being too indecisive in dealing with students. A low score indicates that you do not compromise with your students.

If you scored high in the *abdicator* category, it suggests that you tend to ignore motivational problems. The abdicator is viewed as being reclusive and apathetic toward motivation problems. A low score may suggest that you must confront every incident, no matter how trivial it is.

If you scored high in the *supporting* category, it suggests that you tend to overly accommodate your students when handling motivational problems. It also suggests that you may be overly protective of them. However, supporting a student may be the appropriate style to utilize when the student recognizes his or her problem and suggests a viable solution in resolving it. A low score in this category suggests that you do not have a preference in supporting your students.

If you scored high in the *negotiator* category, it suggests that you handle motivation problems in collaborative and mutual win-win approaches with your students. The negotiator style incorporates both an enforcing and a supporting approach. This style is recommended as being the most effective style to utilize in motivating students.

There may be times when any of these teacher motivation styles may be appropriate for a given motivational situation. Although you should strive to use the negotiator style most often, selecting the most appropriate style for a given situation is the key to effective motivation.

Appendix B

Personality Style Inventory

Directions: For each statement, indicate which response is most characteristic of you in describing your teaching and motivation style. Write a number 4 (*most like you*), 3 (*next most like you*), 2 (*next most like you*), and 1 (*least like you*). This is a ranking. Do not use a number more than once for the five statements.

1. My students tend to view me as
    _____ a. creative and original.
    _____ b. analytical and rational.
    _____ c. personable and empathetic.
    _____ d. pragmatic and assertive.

2. When teaching my students, I tend to be
    _____ a. logical and structured.
    _____ b. more direct and to the point.
    _____ c. warm, sensitive, and insightful.
    _____ d. imaginative and animated.

3. The design of my lesson plans tends to be
    _____ a. creative and innovative.
    _____ b. structured and logical.
    _____ c. personable and student-centered.
    _____ d. practical and direct.

4. When motivating my students, I tend to be
    _____ a. direct and decisive.
    _____ b. casual, patient, and a good listener.
    _____ c. controlled, detailed, and nonemotional.
    _____ d. stimulating and thought provoking.

(continued)

5.   When facing conflict with my students, I tend to be
    _____ a. more emotional, overactive, but personable.
    _____ b. rigid, stern, and controlling.
    _____ c. assertive and perhaps a little impatient.
    _____ d. perhaps a little condescending and opinionated.

Interpreting your scores: Now transfer your rankings (4, 3, 2, 1) on the line provided for each of the following statements. Then add the total for each column at the bottom. Your highest score suggests your dominant personality style, and your second-highest suggests your secondary or backup style. The lowest scores indicate the style that you use the least.

	Intuitor	Feeler	Thinker	Doer
1.	_____ a	_____ c	_____ b	_____ d
2.	_____ d	_____ c	_____ a	_____ b
3.	_____ a	_____ c	_____ b	_____ d
4.	_____ d	_____ b	_____ c	_____ a
5.	_____ d	_____ a	_____ b	_____ c
Total	_____	_____	_____	_____

PERSONALITY STYLES TO MOTIVATE STUDENTS

Teacher style	Approach
Intuitor	Be enthusiastic. Use whole concepts and stimulating ideas. Focus on creativity and constructivism. Brainstorm. Allow flexibility. Be intuitive. Be more qualitative. Allow students to experiment, and give them freedom to experiment.
Feeler	Personalize discussion—be concerned with feelings, uniqueness, and individuality. Approach ideas in relation to past-proven merits. Relate experiences based on emotional reactions and empathy. Consider expression, communication arts, sounds, teamwork, cooperative learning, and group projects. Consider the affective domain of learning.
Thinker	Present instruction in an organized and structured manner. Give alternatives and do not push for immediate action. Be logical and data oriented. Order things in a logical fashion. Be analytical and quantitative in motivating students. Consider numbers, facts, computers, math, science, engineering, systematic inquiry, problem solving, and decision making. Consider the cognitive domain of learning.

(continued)

Doer	Get to the point.
	Talk in terms of the bottom line.
	Be practical and concrete.
	Be spirited and down-to-earth.
	Use physical examples.
	Use the psychomotor domain of learning.
	Allow students to construct and build projects.
	Consider kinesthetic activities, movement, goal-oriented tasks, and utility.

Appendix C

50 Statements to Motivate Students

You're a special student.
Nice job.
I appreciate you.
You're the best.
You're doing a great job.
You are incredible.
Nice work.
Nice progress.
Wow, what good work.
Superb.
That's the best you have ever done.
I'm so proud of you.
You are making significant progress.
Wonderful.
You're on the road to major success.
You're doing very well.
What a nice job.
Perfect work.
Very cool.
That is totally correct.
The best I've ever seen.
Perfect paper.
The top grade in the class.
You're at the top.
You are exceptional.

Wonderful work.
Marvelous.
Tremendous.
Super work.
Great job with this.
You're a great team player.
I respect you.
You are delightful.
Good work as usual.
Spectacular.
Doing fantastic work.
The best of the best.
Wonderful, simply wonderful.
Keep up the good work.
Excellent.
You're on the road to success.
Great improvement.
You keep doing so well.
What an incredible job.
Nice project.
Way to go.
I respect your hard work.
The best I've ever seen on this.
I like your work.
Outstanding, sensational.

Appendix D

Teacher Class Management Survey

The purpose of this survey is to assist you in identifying your strengths and weaknesses in class management.

Directions: Please evaluate yourself on each of the items by circling the number indicating the degree of frequency in exhibiting this behavior with your students.

Frequency scale: 1 = *almost never* 2 = *sometimes* 3 = *frequently* 4 = *very frequently*

Class Management Factors	Frequency Rating			
1. I respect my students.	1	2	3	4
2. I am consistent in administering discipline.	1	2	3	4
3. I regularly motivate my students.	1	2	3	4
4. I have concern and care for my students.	1	2	3	4
5. I expect high performance from my students.	1	2	3	4
6. I am committed to my students.	1	2	3	4
7. I am objective and nonjudgmental.	1	2	3	4
8. I am sensitive and open with my students.	1	2	3	4
9. I regularly praise my students.	1	2	3	4
10. I try to improve the classroom layout.	1	2	3	4
11. I am energetic with my students.	1	2	3	4
12. I am calm and patient with my students.	1	2	3	4
13. I am creative with students.	1	2	3	4
14. I am cheerful with my students.	1	2	3	4
15. I have an open mind with my students.	1	2	3	4
16. I appreciate my students.	1	2	3	4
17. I build the self-esteem of my students.	1	2	3	4
18. I am enthusiastic around my students.	1	2	3	4
19. I understand my school discipline policy.	1	2	3	4
20. I explain my class rules to my students.	1	2	3	4

Total: _____

Scoring: To determine your class management score, add the total numbers. A score of 70–80 = *excellent;* 60–69 = *good;* 50–59 = *fair;* 49 and below = *needs improvement.*

Appendix E

Student Motivation Survey

Name: _____   Date: _____   Grade: _____

Directions: Please rank from 1 to 10 (1 being *most important*, 10 being *least important*) the factors that you feel motivate you to learn.

Ranking	*Motivational Factors*
_____	Good school and classroom conditions
_____	Feeling socially connected with peers
_____	Fair discipline by teachers and administrators
_____	Teacher verbal appreciation for good performance
_____	Tangible rewards (stickers, candy, recognition letters, etc.)
_____	Good grades
_____	Teacher giving encouragement to you
_____	Teacher giving regular feedback to you
_____	Engaging instruction and curriculum
_____	Good classroom management

List any other motivational factors below:

_____
_____
_____
_____

Appendix F

Stress and Motivation Survey

Directions: Answer each of the following questions by marking true or false on the line for each statement.

True	False	Stress and Motivation Statements
____	____	1. I tend to get frustrated with my students' lack of motivation.
____	____	2. I often don't look forward to coming to school.
____	____	3. I feel burned out often during the school day.
____	____	4. I don't exercise enough and stay in good shape.
____	____	5. I often don't eat healthy foods.
____	____	6. I often feel anxious and distracted during the school day.
____	____	7. I find myself lecturing my students to be more responsible.
____	____	8. I find that my students are often apathetic, and this frustrates me.
____	____	9. I often feel my students need to be more motivated.
____	____	10. I often experience disciplinary problems in my classes.

Total: True _____   False _____

Scoring: Add the total number of true answers. If you scored a total of five or more true answers, then you may need to better manage your stress. You might consider reading each statement that you answered true and think of ways to improve your dealing with this item.

Appendix G

Leadership Stress Assessment

Directions: For each of the statements, write the number corresponding to the extent to which you experience the situation.

Scale: 1 = *rarely*   2 = *occasionally*   3 = *sometimes*   4 = *often*   5 = *very often*

1. I feel stressed because of administrative demands. _____

2. There are many financial constraints at my school. _____

3. There are constant increased student performance standards. _____

4. There are constant and unnecessary paperwork demands. _____

5. I feel involved in unending and constant change. _____

6. I am experiencing health problems. _____

7. I am nearing retirement. _____

8. I feel that my job is unfulfilling. _____

9. A loved one has recently died. _____

10. I experience personal financial problems. _____

11. My students are demanding. _____

12. I experience student misbehavior. _____

13. There is student apathy. _____

14. There is high student violence at my school. _____

15. Many of my students have poor academic performance. _____

16. I experience problems with the parents of my students. _____

17. I feel unsafe and insecure at my school. _____

18. I experience conflicting personality differences with people at school. _____

(continued)

19. There are personal conflicts at school.   _____

20. I experience legal and policy problems at school and in life.   _____

Scoring: Add the total number for each of the categories   _____

School stressors (1–5)   _____
Personal stressors (6–10)   _____
Student stressors (11–15)   _____
Work stressors (16–20)   _____
Total   _____

Interpretation: Scores of 18 or higher for each category suggests possible high stress. A total score of 70 or more suggests possible high stress in your life.

Appendix H

101 Motivational Strategies Summary

TANGIBLE REWARD STRATEGIES

1. Letters and certificates of recognition
2. Merchandise, apparel, and trophies
3. Food, treats, and parties
4. Contests, grades, and academic awards
5. Gold stars and stickers
6. Educational gifts and puzzle blocks
7. Self-development rewards

INTANGIBLE REWARD STRATEGIES

8. Verbal appreciation
9. Motivational surveys
10. Enrichment interventions
11. Social needs
12. Good character traits
13. Individual values
14. Coaching strategies
15. Ignore trivial misbehavior
16. Engaging activities

17. Nonverbal messages
18. Adapting to student's style
19. Allow the student to save face

FORMAL REWARD STRATEGIES

20. Scholastic reward
21. Contests and competition rewards
22. Volunteer activities
23. Special events and guest speakers
24. Community recognition
25. Administrator recognition
26. Board of Education recognition
27. Mayor of the City Award

LEADERSHIP STRATEGIES

28. Be responsive
29. Quality and professionalism
30. Serve your customer
31. Collaboration
32. Be proactive
33. Be open-minded
34. Respect diversity
35. Passion and commitment
36. Continual improvement
37. Change your paradigm
38. Self-fulfilling prophecy
39. Moral leadership

DISCIPLINE STRATEGIES

40. Understand defense mechanisms
41. Understanding human needs
42. Rules of behavior

43. Emotional intelligence
44. Punishment
45. Progressive action
46. Discipline styles
47. Discipline by negotiations
48. Tactics and countertactics
49. Establish a vision
50. Establishing good policies
51. Good time management

COMMUNICATION STRATEGIES

52. Be straight with students
53. Avoid scolding students
54. Provide realistic expectations
55. Provide two-way communication
56. Use paraphrasing
57. Use restatement
58. Use close-ended questions
59. Use expanders
60. Use silence
61. Be patient
62. Active listening

STRESS MANAGEMENT STRATEGIES

63. Understanding your tolerance
64. Practice self-talk
65. Enjoy the moment
66. Understand your vulnerability
67. Set realistic goals
68. Externalize your situation
69. Find a useful context
70. Don't be a Typhoid Mary
71. Use positive visualization
72. Think stop

CLASS MANAGEMENT STRATEGIES

73. Drive out fear
74. Organize your classroom
75. Motivational planning
76. Positive use of wall space
77. Effective use of floor space
78. Effective use of storage space
79. Provide necessary safety and security
80. Provide clinical settings
81. Effective task management
82. Be flexible

INSTRUCTIONAL STRATEGIES

83. Good lesson plans
84. Use differentiated instruction
85. Incorporate reflective instruction
86. Provide authentic assessment
87. Use good openings
88. Use good transitions
89. Use effective methods to get attention
90. Providing good facilitation
91. Use humor in your instruction

BUILDING RELATIONSHIP STRATEGIES

92. Begin with hopes, fears, and expectations
93. Building effective teamwork
94. Use concession making
95. Be willing to modify expectations
96. Confront student feelings
97. Keep communications open
98. Initiate collaborative negotiations
99. Mentor your students
100. Developing honesty and trust
101. Care about students, but be skillful

References

Adams, J. (1965). Inequity in social exchange. In L. Berkowitz (Ed.), *Advances in experimental social psychology* (pp. 267–299). New York: Academic Press.

Alderfer, C. (1969). An empirical test of a reference new theory of human needs. *Organizational Behavior and Human Performance, 4*, 142–175.

Algozzine, R., & Jazzar, M. (2006). *Critical issues in educational leadership.* New York: Pearson.

Amends, R. (2003). *Learning to teach.* New York: McGraw-Hill.

Bandura, A. (1977). *Social learning theory.* Englewood Cliffs, NJ: Prentice Hall.

Berne, E. (1964). *Games people play.* New York: Grove Press.

Blake, R., & Mouton, J. S. (1969). *Building a dynamic corporation through grid organization development.* Reading, MA: Addison-Wesley.

Blake, R., & Mouton, J. S. (1985). *The managerial grid III: The key to leadership excellence.* Houston, TX: Gulf.

Boyle, J., & Weishaar, M. (2001). *Special education law.* Boston: Allyn & Bacon.

Brown, A., & Green, T. (2006). *The essentials of instructional design.* Upper Saddle River, NJ: Pearson.

Ciampa, D. (1992). *Total quality.* New York: Addison-Wesley.

Covey, S. (1991). *Principle-centered leadership.* New York: Simon & Schuster.

Curwin, R., & Mendler, A. (1980). *The discipline book: A complete guide to school and classroom management.* Reston, CA: Reston.

French, W., & Bell, C. (1995). *Organization development.* Englewood Cliffs, NJ: Prentice Hall.

Gardner, H. (1983). *Frames of mind: The theory of multiple intelligences.* New York: Basic Books.

Glasser, W. (1965). *Reality therapy: A new approach to psychiatry.* New York: Harper & Row.

Glasser, W. (1990). *The quality school: Managing students without coercion.* New York: Harper & Row. (Reissued with additional material in 1992.)

Goleman, D. (1995). *Emotional intelligence.* New York: Bantam Books.

Harris, T. (1969). *I'm OK—you're OK: A practical guide to transactional analysis.* New York: Harper & Row.

Hendricks, C. (2006). *Improving schools through action research.* New York: Pearson.

Henson, K. (2004). *Constructivist teaching strategies for diverse middle-level classrooms.* New York: Pearson.

Hersey, P., & Blanchard, K. (1977). *Management of organizational behavior* (3rd ed.) Mahwah, NJ: Prentice-Hall.

Herzberg, F. (1966). *Work and the nature of man.* Cleveland, OH: World.

Holm, T. (2002). Humor as a teaching tool: Careful you don't cut somebody. *Teaching Professor, 16*(4), 6.

Jensen, R., & Kiley, T. J. (2005). *Teaching, leading, and learning in preK–8 settings: Strategies for success.* Boston: Houghton Mifflin.

Kilmann, R. E., & Thomas, K. (1977). Developing a forced-choice measure for conflict handling behavior: The mode instrument. *Educational and Psychological Measurement, 37,* 309–325.

Kohn, A. (1993). *Punished by rewards: The trouble with gold stars, incentive plans, A's, praise, and other bribes.* Boston: Houghton Mifflin.

Maslow, A. (1943). A theory of motivation. *Psychological Review, 50,* 370–396.

McGregor, D. (1960). *The human side of enterprise.* New York: McGraw-Hill.

Newman, J. (2006). *America's teachers: An introduction to education.* New York: Pearson.

Oliva, P., & Pawlas, G. (2002). *Supervision for today's schools.* Hoboken, NJ: Wiley.

Romanowski, M. (2005). Through the eyes of teachers: High school teachers' expectations with character education. *American Secondary Education Journal, 34*(1), 6–23.

Rose, L., & Gallup, A. (2005). Thirty-seventh annual Phi Delta Kappa/Gallup poll of the public's attitudes toward the public schools. *Phi Delta Kappan, 87*(1), 41–52.

Sergiovanni, T. (1990). *Value-added leadership.* San Diego, CA: Harcourt Brace Jovanovich.

Snowden, P., & Gorton, R. (2002). *School leadership and administration.* New York: McGraw-Hill.

Starratt, R. (2004). *Ethical leadership.* San Francisco: Jossey-Bass.

Tomal, D. (1997a). Collaborative intervention process: A diagnostic approach for school improvement. *American Secondary Education, 30*(4), 17–24.

Tomal, D. (1997b, October). *Discipline by negotiation: An alternative approach to managing discipline.* Paper presented at the annual meeting of the Midwestern Educational Research Association, Chicago.

Tomal, D. (1999). *Discipline by negotiations: Methods for managing student behavior.* Lanham, MD: Technomic.

Tuckman, B. (1965). Developmental sequence in small groups. *Psychological Bulletin, 63*, 384–399.

Vroom, V. F. (1964). *Work and motivation.* New York: Wiley.

Wagner, T., & Kegan, R. (2006). *Change leadership: A practical guide to transforming our schools.* San Francisco: Jossey-Bass.

Further Reading

Angell, A. (1991). Democratic climates in elementary classrooms: A review of theory and research. *Theory and Research in Social Education, 19,* 241–266.

Augustine, D., Gruber, K., & Hanson, L. (1990). Cooperation works! *Educational Leadership, 47,* 4–7.

Banbury, M., & Herbert, C. (1992). Do you see what I mean? Body language in classroom interactions. *Teaching Exceptional Children, 24,* 24–28.

Brophy, J. (1987). Synthesis on strategies for motivating students to learn. *Educational Leadership, 45,* 40–48.

Brophy, J., & Putman, J. (1979). Classroom management in the elementary school. In D. L. Duke (Ed.), *Classroom management: The 78th yearbook of the National Society for the Study of Education* (pp. 182–216). Chicago: University of Chicago Press.

Burke, K. (1992). *What to do with the kid who . . . Developing cooperation, self-discipline, and responsibility in the classroom.* Palatine, IL: IRI/Skylight.

Cangelosi, J. (1997). *Classroom management strategies: Gaining and maintaining students' cooperation* (3rd ed.). White Plains, NY: Longman.

Canter, L. (1988). Let the educator beware: A response to Curwin and Mendler. *Educational Leadership, 46*(2), 71–73.

Canter, L. (1992). *Assertive discipline: Positive behavior management for today's classroom* (2nd ed.). Santa Monica, CA: Canter.

Charles, C., & Senter, G. (1995). *Elementary classroom management* (2nd ed.). White Plains, NY: Longman.

Corno, L. (1992). Encouraging students to take responsibility for learning and performance. *Elementary School Journal, 93,* 69–83.

Curwin, R. (1980). Are your students addicted to praise? *Instructor, 90,* 61–62.

Curwin, R. (1992). *Rediscovering hope: Our greatest teaching strategy*. Bloomington, IN: National Education Service.

Curwin, R. (1993). The healing power of altruism. *Educational Leadership, 51*(3), 36–39.

Dewey, J. (1938). *Logic: The theory of inquiry*. New York: Holt, Rinehart & Winston.

Evertson, C., Emmer, E., Clements, B., Sandford, J., & Worsham, M. (1989). *Classroom management for elementary teachers*. Englewood Cliffs, NJ: Prentice Hall.

Evertson, C., & Harris, A. (1992). What we know about managing classrooms. *Educational Leadership, 49*(7), 74–78.

Firth, G. (1985). *Behavior management in the schools: A primer for parents*. New York: Charles C. Thomas.

Fraser, B., & O'Brien, P. (1985). Student and teacher perceptions of the environment of elementary school classrooms. *Elementary School Journal, 85*(5), 567–580.

Glasser, W. (1992). The quality school curriculum. *Phi Delta Kappan, 73*(9), 690–694.

Glasser, W. (1993). *The quality school teacher*. New York: Harper Perennial.

Goldstein, S. (1995). *Understanding and managing children's classroom behavior*. New York: Wiley.

Grant, C., & Sleeter, C. (1989). *Turning on learning: Five approaches for multicultural teaching plans for race, class, gender, and disability*. Columbus, OH: Merrill.

Hernandez, H. (1989). *Multicultural education: A teacher's guide to content and process*. Columbus, OH: Merrill.

Hersey, P. (1994). *The situational leader*. New York: Warner Books.

Hill, D. (1990). Order in the classroom. *Teacher Magazine, 1*(7), 70–77.

Jones, J. (1993). *Classroom management: Motivating and managing students*. Needham Heights, MA: Allyn & Bacon.

Kameenui, E., & Darch, C. (1995). *Instructional classroom management*. White Plains, NY: Longman.

Kramer, P. (1992). Fostering self-esteem can keep kids safe and sound. *PTA Today, 17*(6), 10–11.

Macht, J. (1989). *Managing classroom behavior: An ecological approach to academic and social learning*. White Plains, NY: Longman.

McIntyre, T. (1989). *The behavior management handbook: Setting up effective behavior management systems*. Boston: Allyn & Bacon.

Mendler, A., & Curwin, R. (1983). *Taking charge in the classroom*. Reston, VA: Reston.

Mertler, C. (2006). *Action research and teachers as researchers in the classroom.* New York: Sage.

Popham, W. (2006). *Assessment for educational leaders.* Upper Saddle River, NJ: Pearson.

Sergiovanni, T., & Starratt, R. (2002). *Supervision: A redefinition.* New York: McGraw-Hill.

Sharpley, C. (1985). Implicit rewards in the classroom. *Contemporary Educational Psychology, 10,* 349–368.

Slavin, R. (1991). Synthesis of research on cooperative learning. *Educational Leadership, 48,* 71–82.

Slavin, R., Karweit, N., & Madden, N. (1989). *Effective programs for students at risk.* Needham Heights, MA: Allyn & Bacon.

Sobol, T. (1990). Understanding diversity. *Educational Leadership, 48*(3), 27–30.

Tomal, A., & Tomal, D. (1994). Does your economic incentive system really improve quality? *Human Resource Development Quarterly, 5*(2), 185–190.

Tomal, D. (1992). Self-management theory for developing teacher effectiveness: A new pedagogic approach to teacher effectiveness. *Teacher Educator, 28*(2), 27–33.

Tomal, D. (1993). Staff development, filling gaps in teacher preparation. *School Administrator, 50*(2), 51.

Zirpoli, T. (1995). *Understanding and affecting the behavior of young children.* Englewood Cliffs, NJ: Prentice Hall.

Index

About the Author

Daniel R. Tomal is associate professor of leadership at Concordia University Chicago, River Forest, Illinois. He has been a public high school teacher, administrator, corporate vice president, and professor. He received his bachelor of science and master of arts degrees in education from Ball State University, Muncie, Indiana, and a doctorate in educational administration from Bowling Green State University, Bowling Green, Ohio. He has consulted for numerous schools and has testified before the U.S. Congress. While professor at Purdue University North Central, Westville, Indiana, he was voted Outstanding Teacher. Tomal has made guest appearances on such radio and television shows as *CBS This Morning*, *NBC Cover to Cover*, *Les Brown*, *Joan Rivers*, *Tom Snyder*, *The 700 Club*, *ABC News*, and *WYLL Chicago Talks*. He is the author of over 60 articles and research studies and 9 books, including *Discipline by Negotiation: Methods for Managing Student Behavior* (1999) and *Action Research for Educators* (2003), both by Rowman & Littlefield Education.